JET LAG

An Adman's View of the World

BY THE SAME AUTHOR

LE SAUT CRÉATIF, J.-C. Lattès, 1984.
DISRUPTION, John Wiley & Sons, 1996.
HOW DISRUPTION BROUGHT ORDER, Palgrave Macmillan, 2007.

JEAN-MARIE DRU

JET LAG

An Adman's View of the World

pH powerHouse Books Brooklyn, NY

Jet Lag: An Adman's View of the World
© 2011, Grasset & Fasquelle

Originally published in French by Grasset & Fasquelle as *Jet Lag: Le monde vu de la publicité*
Published in English in the United States by powerHouse Books,
a division of powerHouse Cultural Entertainment, Inc.

37 Main Street,
Brooklyn, NY 11201-1021
T 212.604.9074
F 212.366.5247
jetlag@powerhousebooks.com
www.powerhousebooks.com

First edition, 2012

Library of Congress Control Number: 2012936997
Hardcover ISBN: 978-1-57687-617-6

A complete catalog of powerHouse Books and Limited Editions is available upon request; please call, write, or visit our website.

10 9 8 7 6 5 4 3 2 1

Printed and bound in Italy by Graphicom, Vicenza

To Eve
To Samuel

Contents

Introduction

When I fly, I always book a window seat. I never tire of seeing Mother Earth and her landscapes from high above. The ten thousand isles of the Bay of Hong Kong; Mount McKinley rising above the plains of Alaska, the bright green banks of the Nile wending their way through the arid desert; the steep, rutgged uplands of Afghanistan, then Pakistan; all these images will remain forever engraved in my mind. If you want to contemplate the Grand Canyon on a flight from Paris to LA, book a window seat on the left side of the plane.

For more than ten years, my office was in New York. My family lived in Paris. Our biggest agency was in LA. Our biggest client in Tokyo. I spent some of the long hours flying from one continent to the next drafting a few notes on what it is I do and what it is I have done. These intercontinental flights have given me plenty of time to capture my thoughts. This book brings them together. It combines personal souvenirs and anecdotes, reflections and propositions. About advertising, the business world, and the times we live in.

My trade has been like a look-out post, giving me a privileged view of the trends that have marked my time, from the furious growth of globalization to the underground movements of rising generations, the emergence of awareness among businesses of their civic responsibilities, the dreadful handicaps that the world of finance imposes on us, the widely heralded though questionable decline of brands, the shortcomings of marketing, the rise of a new intangible economy, the impact of design on everyday life, the renewed power of word of mouth, the digital-wave practices and products.... Advertising gives us a magnifying glass to observe close-up what influences the life of business, and even sometimes life itself.

I have given this book the form of an alphabet. There is no logical progression from one chapter to the next. It can be read from back to front. The table of contents lets you decide where you want to start, to follow your own path, create your own connections. This format means beginning with our best-known client, Apple, and ending with the campaign that won more awards than any other in the history of advertising, our campaign to save a Zimbabwean newspaper.

Each chapter moves from the specific to the general. I give opinions, but they are always grounded in the particular truth of a product, a brand, a company, a cause, or even a person. I use personal experience to draw general conclusions.

A non-imposed progression from one chapter to another does not preclude a common thread. This book reflects what has been "my life's work" for forty years: encouraging those I meet to always put the most imagination into whatever they undertake.

Apple

"Steve Jobs's passion was to prove everyone wrong," said Lee Clow one evening in January 2012.

Lee Clow is the creative soul of our company. The founder of Apple had just been posthumously inducted into the Advertising Hall of Fame, which was the very least our industry could do. Thanks to Steve, the Apple campaigns conceived by Lee and his teams outdid themselves, campaign after campaign. Remember those black silhouettes dancing against fluorescent backgrounds on iPod posters? The ads that showed us the magical apps for iPads? And that hilarious series of films for Mac versus PC?

Lee had been asked to make the induction speech. I remember well some of the things he said that night. He told us that Steve's vision from as early as the 1980s was that technology was going to change everyone's life, but that this vision was not about business, not about companies, but about people. He wanted to prove that once and for all. Then, emotionally, Lee went on to ask what the world would be like today if Apple hadn't existed. "If Steve wasn't that intense, passionate, uncompromising, maddening perfectionist that he was, do you realize there wouldn't be an Apple, there wouldn't be a Pixar, there wouldn't be a Mac?" He went on: "Steve's intensity just enveloped people and made them want to help accomplish what he wanted to accomplish."

Everything there is to say about Steve Jobs has been said. Every commentator has underlined the fact that he brought about a revolution in five different industries, four of which had nothing to do with his former experience. Nothing surprises people about Apple anymore. In 2011, it became the biggest company in the world by stock market valuation. People now think all this seems so normal. So expected. Except that when Steve Jobs came back to Apple in 1997, almost every stock market analyst was yelling, "Sell!"

Steve Jobs will go down in history as one of the great geniuses of recent times. He was unbelievably inventive. If any other company had just achieved one-tenth of what Apple did, this would have been seen as a breakthrough. But Steve Jobs will be missed for another reason. He offered a beacon of hope in the gray and menacing world that my generation is bequeathing to the next. Steve Jobs showed that a man of no means, starting from nowhere, can make the wildest dreams come true, if only he believes enough. Over and above the fun of surfing with an iPad or downloading music on iTunes, everyone felt something like a ray of hope. That is why Steve Jobs was so adulated.

Steve Jobs's main talent lay in an unusual capacity to give people what they wanted, before they knew they wanted it: a playful computer, a magic phone, a sorcerer's pad. Twenty years ago, our agency in California published a book called *Inventing Desire*. That is what Steve Jobs did. He invented tomorrow's desires. He was the first to sense how a multitude of inventions, often first conceived outside Apple, could be combined into becoming an iPod, an iPad, or an iPhone. He was able to do this because he was incredibly focused. "Innovation has nothing to do with how many R&D dollars you have," he said one day. "When Apple came out with the Mac, IBM was spending at least a hundred times more on R&D. It's not about money. It's about the people you have, how you're led, and how much you get it." Then he added, "People think focus means saying yes to the thing you've got to focus on. But that's not what it means at all. It means saying no to the hundred other good ideas that there are. You have to pick carefully. I'm actually as proud of the things we haven't done as the things I have done. Innovation is saying no to a thousand things."

Over and above the incredible year-in, year-out successes, Steve Jobs left his mark on more than just the businesses he transformed. He brought beauty to a field where beauty was scarcely expected. He turned computers into objects of desire, making design matter. Remember the eighties, when computer science was gray, ponderous, stressful. Then Steve Jobs came onto the scene. He turned computers into giant brightly colored objects or long silver candy bars. He brightened people's offices with compact

Brancusi-like sculptures. He made machines friendly and beautiful.

Jonathan Ive is head of design at Apple, the man Steve Jobs found when he returned to the company in 1997 and to whom he said he owed half of his success. Barely twenty designers work under Ive. That's a tiny number compared with the hundreds of designers working in rival firms. Where does Apple find its unbelievable creative energy? In talented computer engineers and designers, of course. But also in the precision of the demands Steve Jobs and Jonathan Ive made of their teams, and in the briefs they gave them.

Two factors, I suggest, were crucial to these briefs: they insisted on not only the best but also the most intuitive solution to every problem. The first of these criteria goes without saying, but it does mean that working for Apple was like entering a holy order. The second is because for Apple the functions of a state-of-the-art technological product must be easy to grasp. Consumers unsure how something works must be able to find the answer instinctively.

Finding solutions that will be intuitive for others requires a colossal amount of work. Remember the first iPod dial: within minutes, everyone was comfortable with a totally new concept. The company had researched and tested a large number of different systems before settling on a solution so easy that no users' manual was needed. We all know there are no users' manuals in iPhone boxes, either. No other manufacturer has been brave enough to do that.

The Seven Golden Rules of Design

Apple design is peerless. It is exemplary because it obeys the following principles that I would call the "Seven Golden Rules of Design."

You cannot achieve great design if you are just satisfied with minor improvements to existing designs. When the iPod was launched, nothing like it had ever been seen before. It was based on nothing that had been previously produced.

You cannot achieve great design unless design is central to your company. All too often, design is a minor plus, low on the value scale. It serves to cover up for a lack of imagination. The requirement for good design must be visceral.

You cannot achieve great design unless everything within the company, every aspect of it, is integrated. And no company is as integrated as Apple. It is the only firm in the sector to control both hard- and software, the only one where software developers and designers work closely together. At Apple, ideas travel: transversality is exemplary.

You cannot achieve great design unless the production process and design are interdependent. Apple products are not just innovative in the functions they offer, they are also innovative in the way they are made. Apple engineers routinely invent new tools, new materials, and new production processes. Competitors will be slower to copy a product that requires them to manufacture in a different way. Innovative production systems are also a means of keeping the competition at bay.

You cannot achieve great design without an obsessive concern for detail. Look at the finish on an Apple product, and you can see what industrial-scale craftsmanship means. Jonathan Ive once demanded that the blocks of marble destined for the first Apple Store in Manhattan be sent to the head office in Cupertino so he could check the veins in them. Apple has ended up functioning like a luxury goods company. The inside that no one ever sees is treated with as much care as the outside. This is Swiss-watch culture, applied to Silicon Valley.

You cannot achieve great design without allowing for mistakes. Or rather, without actually encouraging mistakes. All artists sometimes end up in a dead end. Jonathan Ive once told *Radical Craft* magazine, "One of the hallmarks of the team is this sense of looking to be wrong. It's the inquisitiveness, the sense of exploration. It's about being excited to be wrong, because then you've discovered something new."

Finally, you cannot achieve great design without aiming for major visual impact. Design is like art. People talk about strong design like they talk about great art. Which is to say, design leaves a mark, just as a great work of art does.

There is currently a renaissance in design. Many years ago, companies like Braun and Sony showed the way. But today few brands exercise as strong an influence over our daily lives as Apple. By giving us beauty where before there was only a kind of "beigeness," the firm has raised our aesthetic expectations.

You can dream of more beauty. You can also demand it. I dream of a world in which every company becomes conscious of the visual impact it creates around itself. I dream that French bank branches will cease bombarding us with their tens of thousands of aggressive Perspex signs, whose neon rays invade our lives at nightfall. I want retailers to bring curves to the bunker-like rectangles of their supermarkets. I want the ugly terraces of Paris cafés to abandon the hideousness they inflict and become inspired by the more contemporary styles of Milan and Budapest bars. I wish town planners would forego populist projects that are polluting the thousand-year-old riverbanks of Europe. I dream that one day our eyes will not have to be confronted with the more than eighty competing signs and panels—I counted them—outside Paris's Gare de Lyon railway station; that modern architects will no longer disfigure our cityscapes. Who could ever honestly defend the atrocious raw green cladding on the new City of Fashion and Design on Paris's Quai d'Austerlitz?

I hope the children in our schools will be taught typography and calligraphy, and that like Steve Jobs, who learned those crafts, they will grow more sensitive to the beauty of material things. Put a plain, sans serif typeface on your storefront, and the value of your business will go up.

Managing Interaction

Working with Apple, I rediscovered that design is not just an aesthetic plus. It lies at the heart of product development. Apple taught us two other important things. They taught us the importance of interaction and—more on this later—the art of reduction.

In 2000, we were told that Apple was thinking of creating its own stores. The aim was to reduce reliance on multibrand retailers who weren't giving Apple the privileged attention it deserved. Apple wanted absolute control over the interaction between Apple customers and Apple. Most especially, Apple wanted to oversee that crucial moment when a customer physically confronts the product, which marketing people call the "first moment of truth."

In the age of the Internet, why would a brand as pristine as Apple want to enter the mundane world of retailing? Surely the right decision would have been to go the Dell route and sell through the Web? Many of us were asking ourselves that question. But one argument made sense to me: in a year's time, Apple was intending to launch a revolutionary new MP3 player (the name iPod was yet to be born). Analysts said it was going to be a hit. They were predicting as much as a 30–40 percent market share, a figure incomparably higher than Apple's plummeting share of the computer market. Once future iPod owners discovered the Apple world, they might think about switching to Mac. But switching from Windows to Mac is a big move. Years of familiarity go down the drain. Apple needed a place where iPod owners could go and try out a Mac computer. These stores help "switchers," as they're known, to spend several hours getting to familiarize themselves with the product before they decide to purchase it.... Mac computer market share has more than doubled since the iPod was launched.

There are now some 380 much-loved Apple Stores in the world. They embody the way product design and store design complement each other. Contemporary marketing is about interaction. From store to product, from iPod to Mac, from iTunes downloads to iPad subscriptions, Apple is a master at interaction. Physicists have long known that managing the interaction between elements increases those individual elements' energy.

In the advertising field, too, the people at Apple are skilled in the ways of managing interaction. They know how a variety of advertising postures work in combination. Leader, challenger, outsider brands all need to adopt a different advertising language. But what if a brand is a leader, a challenger, and an outsider all at the same time?

Until just recently, Apple was an outsider in the computer field; a leader in MP3 players; and a challenger in the smartphone sector. We honed our different campaigns to suit that reality. The computer campaign, for instance, is clearly an outsider campaign. It's a comparative campaign that rests on two characters, one representing Mac, the other PCs.

As *Adweek* put it, "The Mac guy is a younger Steve Jobs who is casual and comfortable in his skin. PC, as a rounder, paler Bill Gates, is a well-meaning geek with all kinds of operating problems." *Adweek* went on to say, "For Apple, the campaign managed the neat trick of making the brand look laid back and cool while it mercilessly skewered its rival." With sometimes innocent but usually devastating wit, Apple was poking fun at Microsoft.

Comparative campaigns are usually outsider campaigns. But market leaders should avoid entering into comparisons. They need to rise above the fray. This is what iPod posters do. The iPod is the unquestioned leader in its sector. The images it offers are imposing. Bold, brightly colored shapes stare down at us from posters. There is no escaping them. In fact, the Mac campaign and the iPod campaign are just about as different as you can get. And yet, their graphic perfection, their simplicity, their beautiful style both speak Apple.

As for iPhones, they came somewhere in between. They had to challenge Nokia and Sony Ericsson. Whereas emphasizing the technical advantages of the iPod would not have been appropriate, the opposite was the case with the iPhone. Focusing on the product, and most especially on its applications, enabled the iPhone to establish a strong competitive edge. And took it from challenger to market leader.

Choosing the right approach to match every product's position in the market helps build brand magic. The way these different approaches interact is priceless; it makes the brand ubiquitous. It means you can become the market leader and still stay cool. That's craftsmanship for you.

Art of Reduction

This brings us to the final lesson Apple taught us: the art of reduction. Let me ask you now to make an effort. Erase all those bright iPod posters from your visual memory. They don't exist. They have never existed. We are in the year 2000. Apple is getting ready to launch a new product that possesses many revolutionary new functions. Everyone says it's going to be a gigantic success, if the launch campaign is good enough. There is a well-known rule in our profession, which says to always highlight the product's exclusive features. The iPod has dozens of them. Now imagine that a young art director comes up with a campaign that seems empty, superficial even. The visuals are just black silhouettes dancing against a range of fluorescent backgrounds. They don't even begin to do justice to the product's exceptionally innovative features.

Many of us failed to see the strength of Apple's great iPod campaign: its iconic dimension. We thought it was superficial and meaningless. We failed to grasp the elegance of its plainness, a quality much cherished by designers. James Vincent, the head of Media Arts Lab, our agency in LA that runs the Apple account, speaks of an "art of reduction." He means the ads apply Jonathan Ive's minimalist approach to advertising.

One of the key aspects of minimalism lies in the duality between simplicity and richness: the pureness of form exposes only the bare essentials. Minimalism's quest for instant comprehension means removing any distraction between an object and what it's for. Apple offers a quintessential instance of this approach. Ornament, superfluous patterns, are set aside. In Apple, we have the object as concept. This is the basis of minimalism in art.

Apple has brought the art of reduction into consumers' lives. This is more than welcome. Today's world is crying out for simplicity. The brand's approach to design has a social corollary. At a time when sustainable development is becoming a decisive factor, where simpler lifestyles are preferred to overconsumption, it seems natural that minimalism should become a strong and positive value, both in economic terms and in society as a whole. It may seem surprising that a brand constantly inventing new consumer needs should be at the forefront of a drive to make things simpler. But that is just one of the many paradoxes of Apple.

Back to Steve Jobs. Several times, during new product launches, he has projected a visual of a street sign at an imaginary intersection between a road called "Technology" and another one called "Liberal Arts." He used this as a description of the kind of multidisciplinary and fertile thinking, sensitive to human needs, that lies at the heart of Apple products. When he launched the iPad in 2010, Steve Jobs stood in front of that same crossroads sign, musing on the secret to Apple's success. "It's in Apple's DNA," he said, "that technology alone is not enough. It's technology married with liberal arts, married with the humanities, that yields the results that make our hearts sing."

Bibendum

"You just made your first mistake," said Jean-Pierre Vuillerme, corporate PR director at Michelin.

The giant global tire-maker, based in Clermont-Ferrand in the middle of France, had always produced its own advertising in-house. But as Michelin expanded internationally, it had appointed agencies in each of the countries where it operated, except France. In 1985 a decision was made to bring France into line with the rest of the world. A competition was organized to appoint an agency for the first time in its home country. We had the pleasure of winning. As is common practice, we requested that a contract be signed. The ensuing negotiations lasted several weeks. And finally, when the time came to sign, Jean-Pierre Vuillerme said to me with a smile, "You don't fully understand this company yet. You've just made your first mistake. Here at Michelin, our word is our bond. A contract can be broken at any time. We will never break our word."

Since that time, our contract with Michelin has been renewed many times, but I'm pretty certain the people we deal with at the company would say exactly the same thing today. Michelin's corporate culture is very deep-rooted and quite unlike any other. As it happens, Jean-Pierre's remark struck a powerful chord with me. My family were food brokers at Paris's Les Halles Wholesale Market. I have witnessed hundreds of deals clinched on just a handshake. Nothing was ever written down.

By mid-2010, our association with Michelin was ready to celebrate its first quarter-century. I made a short speech to mark the occasion. As I was preparing my remarks, I reflected on the lessons I had learned working for Michelin, a firm like no other: old-fashioned in many ways, fundamentally innovative in others.

Most people are interested in cars, but not many are interested in tires. Yet tires play a crucial role in a car's performance, in what makes it safe; in road-holding and braking. Everyday driving subjects tires to a wide range of different tests, from the centrifugal force that comes from cruising on tarmac to the abrasions caused by potholes and bad road surfaces. There's cornering tension, the constant push and pull of the suspension, the sheer weight of the vehicle, severe temperature change, and a whole range of other parameters. A Michelin engineer once told me they had nearly twenty such factors to consider. "Few other manufacturing industries," he said, "have to live within such constraints. The physics is a nightmare."

This may explain the shroud of secrecy that surrounds Michelin's labs. Even François Mitterrand, then president of France, was kept out of some of them when he visited the plant. The fact is, since the nineteenth century, Michelin has shown itself to be the most innovative firm in the sector. The radial tire is a masterpiece copied by every one of Michelin's major competitors. The firm has won exactly one hundred Formula One Grand Prix races. It's a regular rally winner. And if that weren't enough, the space shuttle lands on Michelin tires.

Back in the eighties, though, it was striking that some Michelin work practices hadn't changed since the postwar years. The company was, to put it mildly, frugal. The jargon it uses in-house was and remains somewhat old-fashioned. For instance, instead of calling their reps the "sales force," Michelin referred to them as "The Road." Every morning, "The Road" gathered to meet their area manager at the local post office to get their instructions. (The post office is the only place in France certain to be open at 8:30 a.m. every working day.)

Michelin employees took pride in their work. And every "bib," as Michelin employees are called, believed that anything made inside Michelin, as a matter of course, was better than anything made outside the company. One day, I noticed two people who came to change a window frame at the Clermont-Ferrand HQ. I discovered that both these men were in-house carpenters. The company employed its own in-house craftsmen in every trade. And as I already stated, prior to 1985, even the advertising was designed in-house.

Then we were brought in. Just a few months later, Jean-Pierre Vuillerme called me in to say, "The thing that matters most at Michelin is trust. I would like to inform you that, despite a few minor errors and some misunderstandings, we have come to the conclusion that we are able to trust you. We are appointing you as our agency not just for France but for the whole of Europe as well."

Michelin is a family-managed company that has entered the world league. Along with "progress," "trust" is former chief executive François Michelin's favorite word. I met him only a few times, but I was always impressed by the imposing nature of his presence: a rare combination of stern reserve and openness towards his fellow men. He has a genuine regard for others that lends a warmth to his expression. I knew his son, Edouard, better. He was a man of great curiosity with a twinkle in his eye, who engineered a management revolution to overhaul the company's internal operations. The father had been determined to conquer America. The son considered China to be the new frontier.

It was a driven family that held the reins of the company. François Michelin, though famously prudent, had taken many risks in his desire to conquer the American market. The "boss," as his colleagues called him, knew that his company must go global in order to not fall behind the competition. Without exactly playing double or nothing, he knew at heart that some of the risks he had taken were considerable. Michelin's financial situation, when it bought Goodrich and Uniroyal, might have been a source of concern. In the end, the boldness paid off. Today, Michelin is a world leader.

The taste for secrecy has evolved into a habit of discretion. The company very rarely hits the headlines. Yet in 2010, and again in 2011, the Reputation Institute named Michelin the most respected listed corporation in the Paris Stock Exchange's CAC 40 listing. Even in business circles, not many people know that fact because Michelin will always remain discreet.

Logo of the Century

That didn't stop its logo—its mascot, the Michelin Man—from being elected "Logo of the Century" by an international jury in the year 2000. The Michelin Man's aura spreads far beyond the commercial world. It has inspired painters and sculptors around the globe. It has been copied and parodied in chic galleries from New York's Chelsea to market stalls in the suburbs of Abidjan in West Africa. In France, for more than a century, its nickname, "Bibendum," has been a household word.

Michelin restaurant and hotel guides, as well as Michelin maps, are used by drivers the world over. They know Michelin stars, they understand about measuring the distance between two points from one red "pin" to the next. Tens of millions of us absentmindedly superimpose the signs and symbols of Michelin roadmaps on landscapes we drive through.

Michelin maps enrich our reality. We take a side road, and immerse ourselves in a dash of green that stands for woods and forests. Michel Houellebecq is a mildly outrageous French novelist. In 2010, his most recent novel won France's most prestigious literary prize, the Prix Goncourt. Its hero is an artist who shows blown-up photographs of a Michelin map, taken at a low angle to heighten depth of field. The novel is called *The Map and the Territory*. Its thesis is that maps are actually more interesting than the reality they represent. "The cartography is beautifully complex and absolutely clear. It shows an enchanting territory of dreams," says Houellebecq.

To get back to the Michelin Man, New York's MoMA offered him a prominent position in a show called *High & Low, Modern Art & Popular Culture*. This is how the show's curator described the birth of Michelin Man: "André Michelin and his brother Edouard once visited a stand they had at a trade fair in Lyons. This was in 1897. Edouard, the more artistic of the two, remarked that if you add a pair of arms to a heap of tires, it takes on an appearance of humanity. In early Michelin posters, you can see the transition from industrial product to human form: a man-machine for the age of the motor car." The piece goes on to say, "In the early days, Michelin Man came with a cigar and a monocle, maybe because only the wealthy could afford to drive an automobile. As the campaign developed, he became a 'man of the people.'"

Indeed. Over time, Michelin Man has changed into an almost abstract symbol, an "icon" as people in advertising say. In our business, some brands are referred to as "iconic." If I have given over a whole chapter to Michelin, it is because Michelin's Bibendum—the Michelin Man—is an iconic symbol, skillfully injected into popular culture. The fact is that very few brands attain such iconic status. Coca-Cola, Disney, Levi's, McDonald's, Hermès, Absolut, and more recently.... Apple.

From Brand to Company

Our clients sometimes ask what they must do for their brand to become "iconic." This is a task that implies a shift in public perception and a change in stature. It can be risky: few brands have the necessary standing. I tend to approve the thought, but prefer to offer an alternative route. I suggest treating every brand as if it were a company: the Tide Company, Pampers Company, Nivea Company....

The hierarchical distinction between brand and company may seem overly abstract. In fact, it is useful. It encourages us to think at a different level. It is a way of "institutionalizing" brands. On the one hand, Pampers offers high-quality products— diapers that don't leak—and on the other Pampers generates an iPad app that allows women to watch their baby develop day by day through the nine months of pregnancy. In this way, Pampers acts more like a company than a mere brand. It becomes a catalyst to a whole series of initiatives involving mothers and their babies. Treating a brand as if it were a company

35

clearly gives it additional status. The scope of a company will always be broader than the component elements of a brand.

As early as twenty years ago, I recommended that Air Wick in the US stop its tiresome campaigns to explain that such-and-such a product was three times more effective at removing odors than a competitor and that Air Wick should raise its sights. That Air Wick should become the "air care company," an infinitely more promising starting point from which to expand the brand. I did not succeed. Today, Air Wick still confines itself to claiming that it is better at removing unwanted odors.

The last few decades can be divided into three non-exclusive eras. They are like overlaying strata. First, there was globalization. Then there was the digital revolution. And now we are entering a new era that you could call the "Age of Corporatization." Today, brands are initiating a wide range of concrete actions to justify their new ambitions. At the same time, advertising is broadening its scope. It is operating on a higher plane. This can be a delicate balancing act—on the one hand, "raising" a brand's stature and, on the other, not losing sight of the product along the way. You have to keep shuttling up and down the ladder that connects company, brand, and product.

All the company departments involved with the brand must learn to work closely together. This collaboration is as important as it may be difficult to achieve. There is an unfortunate tendency for each department to think of itself as the brand's sole or primary champion. This obviously causes conflict.

Take the auto industry. Four departments, at least, help define a brand's image in this sector: marketing, design (which is responsible for the physical character of the brand), sales (customer visits to dealers often turn out to be the prime factor in defining a brand), and finally a public relations department, which is essential for an industry that plays a major role in public life. Since the "silo effect" between these four departments is inevitable, one thing becomes obvious. Marketing alone cannot manage the brand, because marketing cannot have precedence over its peers. It can initiate, propose, conceive. It may coordinate. But it cannot decide. The brand is bigger than Marketing.

A company needs to learn how to operate within this context. Work process and decision-making procedures need to evolve in such a way as to ensure that the brand is the yardstick by which things are measured. The brand must inspire. It must bring together. This implies doing two things. On the one hand, a company needs to adopt flat management structures, so that different teams can work more closely together. On the other hand, a higher authority, a "brand champion," needs to be established to arbitrate differences. Because many departments are involved in managing a brand, this brand champion will need to be someone influential, a member of the Managing Board at the very least. In practice most senior managers try to avoid involvement because the idea of "brand" makes them uneasy. They see brands as unmanageable intangibles.

On the contrary, they should see their brands as being too central to be managed by marketing alone. Senior management needs to become actively involved in the process. And when it is, managing a corporation's principal intangible asset—its brands—will achieve the recognition it deserves.

At Apple, it was the CEO who played the role of brand manager for the company. We're all well aware of the results.

Making Truth Bigger

Our job as advertising professionals is to put what companies do in the limelight. Show the value of what brands undertake. Make what they conceive stand out. What advertising does, to quote an expression by French novelist Erik Orsenna, is to "make the truth bigger." Make the truth bigger, a bit like a pair of fingers spreading on an iPad screen to enlarge a photograph.

Our task is to make sure people know Danone is investing in food health, that McDonald's is an active partner in French agriculture, that Adidas is sponsoring basketball courts in socially challenged neighborhoods, that Pampers distributes millions of tetanus vaccines through Africa, that Absolut is responsible for building northern Sweden's Icehotel igloo every winter, that Best Buy offers customers and noncustomers 24/7 help lines over Twitter, that French retailer Super U is helping local employment by supporting locally farmed produce, that Vichy, the skincare company, is offering free dermatological diagnoses over the Internet, that Ikea, the Swedish home products retailer, is setting up wind farms to help offset its stores' carbon imprint, that Nissan and Renault are writing a blueprint for the future by massive investment in electric cars—and since everyone is copying them now, you could say they've provided the world auto industry with several years' progress.

All these facts should be made known to the general public. All these achievements are worthy of being "made bigger." When they are seen as purely commercial moves, people underestimate their significance. When they are "made bigger," people see what they can really mean.

The most valuable brand in the world in twenty years may not yet exist. Just think how quickly Google, Amazon, and eBay have become part of our lives. All the same, over half of the world's fifty most valuable brands are over fifty years old. So there's inventiveness, there's imagination, and there's perseverance, a crucial, if little-mentioned, quality that brings longevity to a brand. Perseverance, determination to hold on to what lies at the heart of a brand: its original culture.

I have spoken of the way Michelin values trust. I have spoken of its discipline. Perseverance is another characteristic trait of this—I was going to say family—corporation. When quality is at stake, Michelin will not compromise. It never has. The position on quality was established from day one. Perseverance remains important to Michelin today, even for what might seem trivial or peripheral matters. Michelin sponsors the Clermont-Ferrand Rugby Football Club, which boasts a massive national record for losing finals. It has lost ten of them. Still, Michelin has never reduced its support. It has stuck with the club, even in its least glorious moments. It has never wavered in its loyalty.

On May 29th, 2010, seventy-four years after Clermont first lost a final, Clermont beat rival Perpignan 19 to 6 in the French National Stadium in Paris to finally win the trophy. The whole nation was watching. The city of Clermont gave the team a heartwarming welcome upon their return. Every single inhabitant was proud. When I discussed the final with Michel Rollier, Michelin's current head, he was lavish in his enthusiasm. May he forgive me if I'm wrong, but I got the feeling this victory meant more to him than the fact that Michelin had won the award for most highly regarded quoted company in France.

At Michelin, what brings people together, what generates shared enthusiasm, will always matter more than external accolades. In-house will always prevail over the outside world.

Culture

"Culture is not part of the game, it is the game."

I often repeat this quote by Lou Gerstner, the former head of IBM. He's famous for turning the corporation around in the nineties, averting a catastrophe many were certain would happen. The comment is especially striking in that Gerstner was trained in the tough school of packaged goods, having spent fifteen years at Nabisco. One might have expected him to be resistant to discussions on intellectual subjects such as "corporate culture."

When he took over, IBM made the move from computer manufacturer to consultant and services provider, then to data management. This was a triple metamorphosis, and yet IBM's culture has remained intact. In fact, it has become stronger.

Culture and business. To many Europeans, this phrase is an oxymoron. The two words don't fit together. On the one hand, few people like business, which seems philistine and too money-focused. On the other hand, everyone loves culture, which is open, accessible, and disinterested. When business people use a word like "culture," they are told they're distorting the meaning of something that is bigger than they are.

Well, I don't agree. The word "culture" is not anyone's to monopolize. In any case, the word has finally come down off the pedestal where some Europeans have tried to keep it. These days we have rock culture, sports culture, web culture. The former head of our digital department recently published a piece entitled *Advertising at the Speed of Culture*. It was about today's popular culture as evidenced by what's on the Internet. The frontier between "high culture" and "popular culture" is fading fast. Indeed, the apostles of postmodernism were proud to boast that they had made the frontier between the two porous.

Founding Acts

A company culture is not born out of nothing. Certain founding acts characterize a business forever from its first beginnings. These come to constitute a thread that runs throughout its history. Such acts help businesses recover from the ups and down of commercial life. They help businesses center themselves, go back to basics, redefine what they are about. I know of very few flourishing enterprises whose success, after a dozen years of activity, does not rest on a series of attitudes and behaviors that were defined in the early days. Business models—the way companies make money—come and go, but culture is lasting. What counts are deliberate decisions and positions established on day one. If these decisions and positions represent a genuine commitment, then they produce a lasting culture. Usually, success ensues.

Take a few well-known French brands. Michelin again, then Danone and Hermès.

Michelin. The laws of physics are such that a tire-maker cannot obtain maximum product performance during the first few miles of a tire's life, as well as maintaining longevity. But car manufacturers, who are tire-makers' largest customers, insist on maximum performance from day one so that trade-magazine reporters can experience optimal road holding during new model trials. Michelin won't go down this route, preferring to sacrifice performance over the first few miles in order to get the best out of the tire over its whole life. One of our campaigns emphasized this approach, that true performance is performance that lasts. Michelin won't sacrifice driver safety for short-term performance. Respect for consumers is the company's core value. It represents the kernel of its culture. If one had to define Michelin culture, one would say: discipline and respect.

Danone. Originally, the company was established to sell fermented milk products to help people's digestion (basically, yogurt). It sold exclusively through pharmacies. This heritage determined the direction taken by the company at the end of the eighties, which you could call "the health axis." Despite launching pleasure products like custards and other creamy desserts, Danone came to understand that it should stick to its original raison d'être and continue to invest in healthy eating. It set up a Danone Institute of Health to provide a better understanding of the connection between food and health. In this way, Danone has funded work by doctors, scientists, and nutritionists. Every year brings new levels of knowledge. Over time, Danone management has set up many related programs. One is the "social enterprise" established with Muhammad Yunus, the founder of the microcredit initiative, to develop nutritional yogurts adapted to the developing world. Programs of this sort show the long-term and deep-rooted nature of Danone's commitment. It is a character trait inherited from Danone's history.

Hermès is a remarkable firm. Its line of conduct is summed up in a quote from a former CEO, Jean-Louis Dumas. "We make goods that are costly rather than expensive." They are costly because Hermès does not compromise on quality. Only the best will do. The brand's coherence over time rests on this approach. Its managers have no interest in changing with the times. Fashion passes. Hermès remains, unruffled by the surrounding hubbub. The goods it makes are beyond question. The finish is perfect. The aesthetics are eternal. "We do not belong to the world of luxury. We do not belong to the world of fashion," commented Jean-Louis Dumas.

Culture is not born from nothing. From day one, Michelin was rigorous about its customers' safety. From the start, Danone's aim has been to sell products that help people stay healthy. From the beginning, Hermès's goal has been to pursue craft excellence without cease. In each case, an uncompromising approach to product hones a corporation's specific culture.

Lessons in Culture

Across the Atlantic, General Electric is known for the stern character of its CEOs and for its fiercely result-oriented culture. It is a tough company that is also amazingly effective. In fifty years, no other company has held so many patents. None has even come close. Gary Hamel, best-selling author of *The Future of Management*, knows why. He says, "General Electric has brought management discipline to the chaotic process of scientific discovery." In his view, it has been this way since Thomas Edison's day. It was Edison who established the industrial research laboratory that laid the foundations for what was later to become General Electric. He did not focus on pure science, but on producing concrete, applied results. He ran his lab like a company. General Electric has respected this legacy. It is an inventive place, ruled with an iron fist. Such is its culture today. The same as it was under Thomas Edison.

Whole Foods sells only organic and natural products. But what has made it so successful is that its products are not aimed just at organic food fanatics. On the contrary. Whole Foods appeals to a broad customer-base. It sells products that, as well as being environmentally friendly and healthy, taste good. Its sales per square foot are twice those of its nearest competitor.... The company's management model is unusual—more like a community than a hierarchy. The internal document that describes Whole Foods's vision of itself is entitled "Declaration of Interdependence." Culture, especially innovative culture, must rest on tangible factors. At Whole Foods, the wage differential between top executive and entry-level employee is ten times less than the US corporate average. Equally, stock options are not limited to a select few: 93 percent of Whole Foods employees have them. Whole Foods was born as a community aimed at customers who, initially at least, belonged to communities of their own. It has succeeded in remaining faithful to its birth certificate.

Running a lab as if it were a business, running a business as if it were a community—these are General Electric and Whole Foods's polar opposite "founding acts."

A strong corporate culture is visible throughout the entire organization. Comparing two mammoth players in the consumer goods field may prove instructive in this respect: Procter & Gamble and L'Oréal are competitors in many markets. The circumstances of their births continue to influence the way they are structured. At the end of the nineteenth century (in 1879 to be precise), Procter & Gamble established one of the first brands in history, Ivory. Already at that time, their motivation for doing this was to redress the balance of power between manufacturer and retailer, by creating consumer demand. Procter & Gamble invented the "brand manager" concept. As a result, the corporation is still structured into major divisions, each including homogenous product categories, based on leading brands like Tide, Olay, or Pampers. It has a Soap Division, a Skincare Division, a Paper Division, and so on.

Eugene Schueller launched L'Oréal by selling hair dye products to hairdressers. Hairdressers, and then the other circuits of distribution, made the company what it is. L'Oréal is structured around a series of major divisions, too. But unlike Procter & Gamble, its divisions are client based: perfume stores, pharmacies, general retailers, and hairdressers. At Procter & Gamble the brand is more important than the distribution circuit. At L'Oréal it is the other way round...Until recently, organizing any other way than by brand was debatable. But as retail distribution circuits merge into giant corporations, L'Oréal's approach has given it an increasing competitive advantage.

Other parallels, or rather differences, between Procter & Gamble and L'Oréal jump to mind. Perhaps they reflect a contrast between the former's midwestern culture and the more European culture of L'Oréal. Procter & Gamble stresses the scientific aspect of its skincare products when they are sold through pharmacies and their beauty aspect when they are sold in perfume stores. Coherence is what matters. The thinking is single-minded. L'Oréal, on the other hand, knows that the key to successful sales lies in the combination of science and beauty. Its approach is consequently subtler. It emphasizes a dimension that may seem out of sync with the distribution channel used. In beauty stores, the scientific aspect is talked up. Conversely, in pharmacies, products are given a beauty bonus angle. Procter's is the single-minded approach. L'Oréal prefers the more complementary route.

The same contrast appears in decision-making procedures. Again, Procter & Gamble's approach is straightforward. The way the company has been run focuses on a sacrosanct "recommendation" system that makes its way step-by-step up the corporate ladder from brand manager to CEO. A recommendation is accepted or rejected according to the analytical rigor upon which it is founded. This approach hardly encourages unbridled discussion. L'Oréal, on the other hand, likes to arrange "confrontation meetings," as they are officially known, in which opposing arguments are debated by a range of managers to help the boss make the best possible decision.

Both these cultures are homogenous, you might say holistic. They have evolved their own internal logic and thus come to influence management structure and behavior over time. As my psychology teacher in college used to say, structure determines behavior, and behavior determines structure. L'Oréal and Procter & Gamble have illustrated this principle from my early years.

Strong corporate culture provides people with a framework within which to work. The things they do every day make more sense. A job becomes more than just a job. Culture builds bridges between colleagues, regardless of what department they belong to, what status, or what nationality they hold. Culture provides a collective goal. It offers cohesion.

David Maister, a former professor at Harvard Business School, has produced research to demonstrate the competitive advantage strong culture offers. In analyzing over one hundred companies, he has identified a clear correlation between job satisfaction and financial results. He has established that companies that develop strong internal culture enjoy greater employee satisfaction, and companies that offer employees greater job satisfaction are more profitable. In other words, a company's internal culture is the most significant factor behind employee morale, and employee morale is what most influences profit.

Some people remain skeptical. They point out that placing too much respect on corporate culture can be inhibiting. They see a tendency to hide behind safe-haven values, to seek reassurance in predictable patterns of behavior. Company culture, in this instance, they say, can hinder change.... Maybe, but in practice, company culture also helps companies to transform themselves. The times we are living in demand greater business mobility. Businesses' capacity to react positively to a crisis is directly proportionate to the strength of the values they share with their employees. In a turbulent world, a strong corporate culture helps companies deal with all kinds of change without losing their identity along the way.

Good Enough is Not Enough

Culture matters at TBWA, too. We work in a highly competitive environment. Any newcomer to advertising can set up shop and within just a few weeks compete with established agencies. Few markets are as open to competition as ours is. There are no barriers to entry. According to John P. Kotter and James L. Heskett, the authors of *Corporate Culture and Performance*, the work of reference in this field, the impact of a company's culture increases according to competitive intensity. Which is why I think ours is so crucial. Our culture is based on a series of principles. I've counted twelve. They shape the way we work. Wherever I go within the worldwide network, I always remind people how specific our culture is. I'm a missionary of sorts, spreading the good word about what our group believes in. From Kuala Lumpur to San Francisco, I spell out the principles. I am convinced that at the end of the day, they will bring us two or three extra growth points and make all the difference.

A statement by Jay Chiat, the founder of our LA agency, is visible on the walls in many of our offices: *Good Enough is Not Enough*. Easy to agree with this statement. But try putting it into practice every day, and you'll see it's a real challenge. Not settling for whatever's just "OK" turns out to be a relentless and demanding exercise....

The other principles I talk about when I travel around our network describe our methods, our business

50

model, our way of building our businesses plans. In every case, my goal is to stress what is distinctive about our approach. I go on to analyze the way we communicate among ourselves, train people, look for new clients, build relationships with our suppliers, and commit to charities. I list some of the key words in our vocabulary, which profoundly reflect this culture of ours. And finally I explain how it is we are trying to influence the future of our industry.... Eleven points so far.

The twelfth point covers a general evaluation of performance. What tool should we be using? Tom Carroll, my close friend and successor as network CEO, has changed our system of reference. We no longer think it's enough to establish comparisons with the direct competition. We want to be one of the most innovative companies in the world, across the board. When we tell reporters this is our goal, they sound surprised. They know we already rank among the most creative advertising networks. Some years, we even came in first. But now we want to compete regardless of sector. This changes our system of evaluation. We no longer refer to creativity as defined by advertising festival awards, even though we are still delighted to collect them. We mean something different by creativity. We mean innovation in a wider sense, in terms of how we see our company. From now on, our role might consist in creating a new iPad app. It might be to devise a new brand architecture through a fresh approach to design.... Overnight, the nature of the competition has shifted. The groups we measure ourselves against now are called Apple, Disney, Nike, Google, and Amazon.

As a goal, this may sound presumptuous, but it's a way to take us higher and further. Indeed, we were the first advertising network to be listed among the most innovative companies in the world by *Fast Company* magazine. We ranked twenty-fourth, behind Apple, Disney, and Google, but ahead of Microsoft, Toyota, and Nike. Staying up there is tough, but making it a goal has brightened our horizon.

I have been teaching in French universities and graduate schools for a long time. I teach at HEC, the leading French business school. And at the Sorbonne, Paris's nine-hundred-year-old university. Many of the students I see are sick of their business studies routines. They want me to provide advice that is "disruptive." They believe I have developed a series of unconventional rules of management. Well, I haven't. Not really. But I do offer this paradox: to me, the hardest thing to handle in business is not disagreement, it's soft agreement. Lazy consensus.

Where there's active disagreement, someone has to settle the differences. A direction is given. Opponents will be brought into line. But where there's soft consensus, people become disengaged. They may think they're on the same wavelength, but they don't all put the same energy into what they do.

Agreement of this sort is stress-free. It's easy to live with. It covers issues people never discuss, because agreement is taken for granted. When asked, "Does management culture matter?" two executives may both reply in the affirmative. But maybe the first thinks business culture is critical to success; the second that it's important but not vital. If the latter moves up the corporate ladder, the business will gradually slip. When hiring someone to fill an important position, faced with two similar candidates, his preference will not be the same. Investment priorities will be subtly different, too. Almost imperceptibly, a different company will come into being.

In the seventies and eighties, I witnessed the rise of big, beautiful international advertising agencies with admirable company cultures. Over time, they wasted away, succumbing to rampant banality. If you're not careful, any company will gradually subside in this way. The tendency is no less pernicious for being invisible to the naked eye. Culture slippage is always fatal.

Every morning when I go to work, I think about our culture. And I hope my successors will do the same.

Disruption

"Disruption is our unfair competitive advantage."

Carisa Bianchi is CEO of our LA agency, the most influential office in the network, employing close to one thousand people and coordinating many global clients such as Nissan, Visa, and Apple. The agency's reputation for creativity has been at the top for four decades. I've often quoted Carisa's saying, "Disruption is our unfair competitive advantage." By "unfair," she means Disruption is our trump card, the not-so-secret weapon our competitors envy. To her, Disruption breaks the rules by which advertising professionals usually play.

I often use the concerted attack orchestrated by players from the English-speaking world against the French wine industry as a perfect example to illustrate Disruption. What happened was non-French wine producers succeeded in convincing their English-speaking customers that grape variety (Cabernet, Merlot, and so on) matters more than provenance (Bordeaux, Burgundy, etc.) Suddenly, wine lists in

London and New York were turned upside down. French wines became just a speck in a plethora of Chilean and Australian wines. A relatively simple disruption was brought about by shifting viewpoints. But it had a devastating impact on French winemakers. Their products are no different to what they always were. How could they be? The only thing that changed is how the market is defined. Which makes it such a neat example.

Disruption occurs when there is a before and after in the life of a brand. When a break, a hiatus occurs. At a given point, the brand or the company is no longer seen in the same way. It is a pivotal moment.

We have had the fortune to contribute to a great many disruptions. We helped transform a vodka brand into a contemporary arts sponsor; a video-game console into the symbol of an industry that has come to rival Hollywood; a brand that sold food for dogs into a company obsessed with everyday dog well-being, and leading to the creation of the world's greatest dog adoption drive; a telecom operator into a company for "doers," for busy people who don't have time to waste talking too long on the phone; we have helped turn sports watches into luxury watches, the leading American fast-food chain into an active part of European society, a tired runner-up in sports shoes into a combative challenger, an Asian bank into an ethical and respected enterprise, gardening products into a cosmetics and beauty line for plants, clothes produced in prisons into fashion items, a Japanese chewing-gum brand into an aid to concentration;

we transformed SUVs into urban-proof cars, dairy products that taste good into products that do you good. We invited youngsters to "taste the rainbow." We said "every generation refreshes the world," we told people "not everything in life that counts can be counted," or again that "envy is ignorance and imitation is suicide." We showed that it is not up to people to adapt to computers but for computers to adapt to people. And so we promised that 1984 won't be like *1984*, and fifteen years later, again for Apple, we wrote just two words, two words that are an invitation to create Disruption everywhere: "Think Different."

First Steps in a New Method

I've often been asked where the idea for Disruption came from, how did it come about? The method and the word to describe it first appeared in 1991. But that was the end result of a long process that began with my first week at work. I owe a great deal to my boss at Dupuy Compton, the first agency I ever worked for. When I asked him what an account executive's main task was, he gave me a surprising answer. I had been expecting him to tell me about client satisfaction, about respecting deadlines and budgets or even—Dupuy was recognized on the creative festival circuit—the ability to sell unusually daring campaigns. But he didn't. He said, "Write good briefs." Then he added, "A good brief may produce a good campaign. Not infallibly, but sometimes. A bad brief always produces a bad campaign. Over a period of years, no one will change a good campaign. They'll just update it. This means spending less time than in year one. And this will end up delivering more profit." He taught me the direct correlation between good campaigns and profit. He told me that in what are now called creative industries, creativity underpins rigorous, disciplined management.

Every summer, advertisers from the world over make their way to the French Riviera to celebrate the best campaigns of the previous year. This is the Cannes Advertising Festival. The movie festival happens in May. Ours happens in June. The general public doesn't know this, but it does bring together some ten thousand people, including more than five hundred reporters. I first chaired this festival in 1982. I was honored to have among my jury Martin Boase, who ran the British agency that established the first "strategic planning" department in history. Believing, like my first boss, that designing the brief is a key moment in the life of a campaign, he established a department specifically to that end. His firm, BMP, employed as many planners as account people. Their role was to represent the consumers internally, to anticipate their needs and analyze their prospective reaction to campaigns still in the conception stage. Each planner would organize several group sessions to explore the potential of each campaign. His job was not so much to judge ideas for campaigns, which might have led to some being eliminated, as to identify key points on which creative staff might expound.

Struck by the fact that his agency kept winning Golden Lions with remarkable constancy, I asked Martin Boase to lunch so that we could have a long conversation. I wanted to know how he did it. When I asked what the roots of this creativity were, he replied, "Strategic planning." This confirmed what I had always suspected, but applied in a disorganized way. The creative imagination soars when it can rest on solid foundations, in other words on strong and thorough planning work that transforms a client brief into an inspirational brief founded on the same information. Such is the job of strategic planning.

A brief will always prove more effective if, as for Absolut, it can go beyond stating the brand's origins and heritage to suggest treating vodka as a work of art; if it is conducive to setting up not just a campaign but a program, as in the "Pepsi Refresh Project"; if it can help Adidas explain that every sports person believes their personal record to be insuperable until the day they beat it; and if it can encourage Apple to put aside the technical characteristics of its products to make it a brand that epitomizes a digital lifestyle.... There are a thousand different ways of talking about brands. What counts is a new perspective; revealing unacknowledged behavior; challenging conventional attitudes; making a paradox work; or maybe introducing some new strategic idea.

That lunch in Cannes was a turning point in my life. Since that time, I have become obsessed with the importance of briefs. In some ways, this obsession has set the agencies I've run apart. I keep saying writing a brief is not about transmitting existing information. A brief is an act of invention.

Convention, Disruption, Vision

Near the end of the eighties, we set up an international network based in Paris called **BDDP**. This company, as we will see later, eventually merged with **TBWA**. Nick Baum, our network's international president, insisted that the network establish a standard working method of its own. I found this puzzling. Agency methodologies seemed restrictive, belittling—anything but inspirational. To me, writing a brief is a creative act. It has to be different every time. The very way in which a strategic goal was described needed to change according to each case. Four or five years spent working with this freedom had produced memorable campaigns at a national level. Just two decades after France's May 1968 cultural revolution, we were living through an exhilarating period. The economic and social context had altered a great deal, but somehow the spirit of the sixties was back.

Acquiring agencies internationally to establish a global network marked a turning point for us. Suddenly, it was indeed obvious that we needed a formal framework to establish a common language between all these new agencies across different countries, among people of dissimilar backgrounds. We needed to establish a new way of working together, a way that would encourage the development and propagation of our own methodologies.

In the early days of **BDDP**, many of our clients gave us briefs for brands that were in trouble. So this became our specialty. We told clients, "Give us your most difficult brand." In a tight spot, even a desperate one, we always came up with a daring, risky response. The French expression we coined to describe what we were doing was *stratégie de rupture*. This was a way of going deeper and further into the old idea of breakthrough.

Early in 1991 the director of strategic planning at the New York agency we had just acquired asked me that classic question people put when they are seeking to establish corporate identity: "What do we stand for?" I explained what we meant by *stratégies de rupture*. She saw the relevance of our approach, but the word "rupture" was a stumbling block. In French, rupture implies an invigorating break with the past. In English it implies a painful medical problem. So she came up with a variety of other possible terms, among which was the word "disruption." At the time, this was used only in a negative sense, to describe something problematic or perturbing. Despite the unpleasant connotations, I adopted it to describe how we operate.

A concept was born. At first, everyone said we'd chosen a really clumsy word. Anyway, what was the point of coining a new methodological term for something we were doing instinctively? We were not deterred. With the strategic team in New York, we perfected our new tool. This would soon prove its usefulness in a thousand and one different ways, first and foremost in creating a culture and language common to our entire network. In May 1992, a full-page ad in the *Wall Street Journal* heralded the launch of our new approach. A one-word headline,

"Disruption," and fifteen hundred words of text to describe the process. Disruption took off.

In the beginning, there were a few anxious moments. Many were skeptical. And they were right. Our early writings on the subject were unnecessarily complicated. Paul Bainsfair, the then head of our London agency, was never slow to crack a practical joke. At a network convention of two hundred colleagues from around the world, he projected that famous bit from Monty Python's *Life of Brian* where Graham Chapman, playing Brian, pokes cheeky fun at the self-important preachers who bore us with their doctrines and their dogmas. Today, more than fifteen years later, I still don't know whether this mockery was an attempt on the life of Disruption or, on the contrary, a means of overcoming the ambivalence toward its adoption.

Despite these teething troubles, our new method gradually found favor. People discovered that Disruption was not a traumatic constraint, but a tool that made everyone's job easier. Chapters in several books were written about it. Clients liked it. It attracted notice from professionals outside our agency. Nowadays, the basic textbook on Disruption has been translated into twelve languages and has sold very well. Even if some tens of thousands of copies were a pirated Chinese version. Flatteringly, Tom Peters, author of *In Search of Excellence*, described Disruption as one of "the most powerful ideas in business today." Perhaps a slight overstatement.

In 2003, the invention of Disruption Days helped to make Disruption operate as the method we now know. These "Days" bring together about twenty people from every department in our agency, with a similar number from every department in the client firm: Sales, Manufacturing, Finance, Legal Affairs, as well as Marketing. We also invite people from Head Office, who mix with junior executives. It is important that every level in the hierarchy is represented. We have organized some three thousand Disruption Days through the network. More than fifty thousand client representatives have already participated.

John Hunt, who co-founded with Reg Lascaris our agency in South Africa, is the inventor of the Disruption Days process. These are planned around the Convention-Disruption-Vision sequence which lies at the heart of our method. We start the day by examining market conventions—all those things that have become invisible because they are so familiar. By the end of the morning and in the early part of the afternoon, we devise ways of disrupting these conventions and upsetting the established order. Then, a succession of exercises enables us to come up with or explore a long-term vision for the brand....

When the heads of our LA agency realized what John had developed, they immediately adopted and sophisticated the process. You can't take part in a Disruption Day at our LA office without being profoundly affected by the experience. Weeks, sometimes months, of preparation go into it. The office is taken over. Eight meeting rooms are covered in paperwork and flip charts and summaries. Some become "Convention Rooms." Others "Vision Rooms.'" Participants are split into four groups. They move from one room to the next according to a pre-established narrative.... Thirty or forty people can show unsuspected creativity providing no distinction is made between those that are professionally creative and those that are not. As Gary Hamel says, "It's time to stop creative apartheid." Which is where Disruption Days come in. They make it possible for everyone's imagination to shine.

You don't emerge completely unscathed from this experience. Most of our clients devote all their energy to a brand and its products. Seeing that brand's everyday environment taken to pieces is an experience most wish to repeat. Some want Disruption Days organized every year.

Moving Faster than the World We Live in

Disruption is connected with the notion of discontinuity. It rejects gradual change, rejects marginal improvement, rejects "incrementalism." In my first book, *The Creative Leap*, I wrote that creative talents must make a leap of the imagination in relation to existing strategy. Being satisfied solely with words that rephrase the strategy is not enough. Even with the addition of a catchy slogan, this does not make up for the lack of an idea. An idea is something that transports us elsewhere. Hence the expression "creative leap."

Disruption represents a move from the creative world to the strategic world. The leap takes place at the strategic stage, even before the creative process has begun.

For many years, letting the imagination loose at the strategic stage was just unacceptable. Identifying strategic relevance was considered difficult enough. At Procter & Gamble especially, using the word "creative" in relation to strategy was blasphemous. Strategy was only about relevance.... Disruption breaks down the barrier between strategic thinking and creative expression. We say: imagination is required at every stage of the process, upstream and downstream.

Some believe that Disruption aims for the impossible. That it is the fruit of presumptuous minds, ill mannered enough to believe that they can define rules for innovation. What is the sense in claiming to take a stand against preset formulas if at the same time one appears to be offering a new type of formula? The notion of "Disruption" is self-contradictory: How can one create disorder in an orderly manner? Peter Drucker has a good answer to that: "Creative destruction needs to be an ongoing process, and it has to be organized." There has to be a framework within which to think, an organized approach to problems. This is why we always start out by researching market convention, the received wisdom on how things are done. Why we always follow a succession of pre-established procedures, each of which is the product of non-variable exercises and questionnaires.

There is also a matter of obsolescence; of overfamiliarity. Not many agency methodologies or approaches have lasted so long. Everyday I hear things like, "Disruption's been around for twenty years. Our business is about novelty. Isn't time we moved on?" Or maybe, "Wasn't Disruption developed at a time when mass media were still at their height, a time when every brand needed to focus on one message, and isn't that at odds with the more fragmented expectations of a digital age?" The answer to both questions is no. Innovation will always be about challenging conventional attitudes. Every domain has its own logic. Every era generates its own dominant modes of thought. One conventional wisdom succeeds the next. Any young artist wanting to have an impact has to upset the codes of the previous generation. Every scientific breakthrough involves challenging a widely accepted recent theory. Disruption is to commercial disciplines like sales, marketing, and communication what innovative minds have always achieved in the wider world.

Nonetheless it is true that Disruption must not rest on its laurels. It mustn't grow stiff. It must not become a series of rigid prescriptions. Nothing is beyond being challenged. Nothing is sacred. We have always wanted Disruption to be an organic method that grows richer through the accumulation of experience in thousands of Disruption Days. And this is in fact happening. The method is evolving month by month. It's alive.

Indeed, the word "Disruption" itself has renewed its meaning. Originally negative, it has gradually come to take on a positive sense, at least in the world of business. Commentators use it more and more. They speak of disruptive strategies and programs. They use the term "Disruption" with a capital *D*. Over the years, our role as creators of the concept may even be forgotten. A reporter for *Executive* magazine in the US, probably barely thirty years old, recently accused me, during an interview, of illicitly appropriating a notion that had circulated for years. As far as he was concerned, there was no way Disruption could have been invented so recently. It had to be a strategic method long since passed into the public domain. A.G. Laffley, former Procter & Gamble CEO, and Jim Stengel, former global marketing officer at the same corporation, must believe this, too. They've been using the term "disruptive innovations" for five years now. This is the key expression in a book by the former entitled *The Game Changer*. Techcrunch, one of the world's most popular tech blogs, recently acquired by AOL, organizes a one-day seminar each year about the most innovative start-ups. And what is this seminar called? "Disrupt".... And at the end of the year, *Business Week* elects the "Disruptors of the Year." So it looks like we are going to lose the battle for ownership of a concept we created.

From an advertising method, Disruption became a marketing tool, then a catalyst to accelerate business. It is a "problem-solving" technique of sorts. Convention-Disruption-Vision, as a sequence, helps find solutions in areas way beyond just advertising. It is a method that has allowed us to bring innovation in activities as diverse as searching for new retail circuits, setting new recruitment criteria for HR departments, establishing R&D priorities, finding new approaches to diversification, conceiving briefs for investment analysts, or rebuilding cultural bridges after a merger.... We've even organized a Disruption Day for a law firm.

In Finland, we did a Disruption Day for government. Finland is a small country. Its economic health is primarily dependent on Nokia. What to do when Nokia's world leadership position drops following injudicious strategic decisions? Government is not competent to influence a private corporation's strategic choices, but it can subsidize alternative and promising sectors. We helped the Finnish authorities identify a few avenues. In Thailand, many businesses come to us to find new business models. They are feeling the squeeze of Chinese brands on one side, Indian brands on the other; all are more famous, often offering better products at more competitive costs. Wherever we are—Helsinki, Bangkok or elsewhere—we try to broaden the horizons of those who come to us for advice.

Over the last twenty years or so, companies have gradually become used to the idea of permanent change. The idea isn't scary any longer. But in 2008 economic crisis arrived. Recession forces sudden and unexpected turns. In the new context, the meaning and purpose of Disruption have evolved. Disruption may not always initiate change, but it knows how to encourage it. It teaches how to use unpredictable developments as a way forward. It provides a definitive answer to the question "Is the company changing as fast as the world it lives in?" When this issue arises, I tell clients to arrange Disruption Days. When they ask why, I give them the obvious reply: "Changing everything is an invitation to failure. Changing nothing is, too."

Then I add, "Deciding what to change is the hard part. That's what Disruption's for."

Efficiencies

"Death Spiral" is the title I gave a piece I wrote for *Advertising Age* about the decline in agency fees.

Our profession has never been good at establishing fair remuneration. The reason is simple. We sell ideas. But we are unable to assess their worth. This difficulty is not restricted to advertising. It affects all cognitive industries, industries of the mind that lie at the heart of the new century. None of us knows how to quantify intangibles.

The chairman of the Association of National Advertisers read the piece in *Advertising Age*. He invited me to his annual convention, in Boca Raton, FL. The audience was made up of four hundred procurement representatives. Most of them were not going to be in agreement with what I was going to say. So to set the ball rolling, even if that meant raising a frown or two, I started off with an Oscar Wilde quote lambasting "people who know the cost of everything and the value of nothing."

When asked about fees, Neal Grossman, our LA office's COO, starts off showing a short movie. Basically, over the last twenty years advertisers have made hourly rates the most common basis for calculating remuneration in our business. Labor costs are calculated on the basis of the amount of hours worked, a bit like a cab driver and his meter. The movie is an attack on this inadequate and unfair approach. The year is 1927. The place, Stonestreet Studios, Hollywood, CA. Mr. Stonestreet sits at an impressive desk wearing thick spectacles. His guest is a Mr. Disney, who stands. Mr. Stonestreet offers to "buy" a character created by Mr. Disney called Mickey Mouse. Stonestreet congratulates Disney on his work, then immediately asks him how long it took to devise the character. Mr. Disney does not understand the question. He does not see that Mr. Stonestreet is interested in knowing how long it took to devise Mickey Mouse in order to arrive at a price. The rest of the conversation continues in the same vein of incomprehension, on how many hours were spent drawing. Mr. Disney remains courteous, even deferential. But he cannot conceal his astonishment at Mr. Stonestreet's approach. Finally, the latter counts out seventeen hours' worth of work, at a rate of five dollars an hour. He will not negotiate either the time involved or the hourly rate. He offers the sum of eighty-five dollars for an invention that will make hundreds of millions and enchant generation upon generation of human beings.

In this picture, Mr. Stonestreet talks only in figures. Mr. Disney, on the contrary, explains how he came to draw Mickey Mouse, how the idea sprang out of nowhere. This expresses the intangible dimension. The gap between the two discourses underlines the futility of reducing the worth of an idea to the number of hours involved in having it. Mr. Stonestreet of course does reach a price. But the price bears no relationship to the value of what he is proposing to purchase....

This problem affects all creative industries. In his book, *How Much is an Idea Worth?*, French author Marc Halévy emphasizes that "the rise of the intangible economy has brought about a divorce between price and value." There is a need to find ways of bringing the objective world, as reflected in purchase price, into line with the subjective world, which relates to the value of what is purchased.

Back to advertising. The pressure on revenue can be partly explained by recession, partly by the digital revolution that has turned our working habits upside down. But the dominant factor remains the increasingly vociferous presence of procurement professionals. Management keeps asking them for more. More and more. So they have to whittle every budget down to the last cent, hunt for greater and greater "efficiencies," keep coming back week after week, day after day. Soon, more time will be spent discussing how we get paid for our ideas than finding those ideas.

Over the last few years, we've fallen beneath a viability threshold. We now have to come up with campaigns in just a few days. By comparison, L'Oréal or Ford's engineering department takes two to three years to develop a new product. The imbalance is not right. Dozens, maybe hundreds, of people's work is going to be made the most of, or damaged, by a creative team of two or three who won't be able to give the task enough time. I see the effects of the stranglehold every day. No agency dare denounce the situation openly in case they become accused of being ill managed. But all the people in the business know the hole we've gradually allowed ourselves to be trapped in.

We're not good at defending ourselves. A management consultant from McKinsey, BCG, or Bain, at similar levels of seniority and training, is paid twice as much per hour as someone at management level in advertising. The gap is not justifiable on fundamentals. Management consultants' economic model is much more profitable than ours because they often provide prefabricated recommendations. They are off the shelf, ready-to-wear. Ad agencies' are custom made. I see what management consultants offer. I know what we bring....

Creating Value

A small vodka brand dropped by in 1981. It wasn't even Russian. Thirty years and eight hundred print ads later, Absolut ranks second in the world league of vodka brands and fourth for all liquors. In this instance, the value created can be measured in monetary terms. French liquor giant Pernod Ricard bought Absolut from the government of Sweden in 2008 for nine billion dollars.

When the owners of Tag Heuer hired us to run their advertising, they were selling sports watches for an average of six hundred dollars. Three years later, having refreshed their design and benefited from a "Don't Crack Under Pressure" campaign, the average price of the watches was nearly twice as high, at $1100. Shortly afterward, the company was listed on the Swiss stock market. The listing was a spectacular success for shareholders. Since that day, Tag Heuer is taught in business schools as a classic example of moving upmarket. Tag Heuer now rivals luxury brands.

In 1990, we recommended that Danone establish a "Danone Institute of Health." The consequences are still making themselves felt, two decades later. Sometimes, the success of a new initiative becomes the absolute confirmation of the relevance of the strategy. This was the case here. Today, two-thirds of Danone's sales are attributable to products like Actimel or Activia that are health orientated. Twenty years ago, two-thirds of Danone's sales came from sweet and dessert-type products. Reviving the brand's origins in health gave it a new lease on life.

These examples teach us something crucial. How can you assess the value to Danone of a strategic recommendation whose effects have made themselves felt over two decades? What proportion of the nine billion dollars Absolut was sold for in 2008 is attributable to its agency, knowing that advertising has been responsible in a major way for the brand's achievements? That day down in Florida, I also mentioned Adidas. How can you value the in-house impact of a rallying cry like "Impossible is nothing"? To what extent did it renew sales team spirit, given that Adidas's representatives had to confront Nike everywhere they turned? I also mentioned SNCF, the French state railways. How do you determine the value of a TV campaign for their freight division, when you know that its real effect was to dissuade workers from launching a financially crippling strike?

The difficulty is that there is often no way of measuring the value of what we produce. So our clients end up ignoring it.

Three Paradoxes of Remuneration

In procurement, what can't be measured does not exist...which is why procurement only assesses performance in terms of cost reduction, never in terms of added value. Creating value is not quantifiable to any degree of accuracy. The only thing that interests companies' procurement is what they call "efficiencies." That day in Boca Raton, I came up with the first of three paradoxes: "The part that matters most is the part you don't pay for."

I asked a series of questions. The Internet makes it possible for an idea to become its own medium. When that happens, surely it makes sense to reward not just the idea, but also its ability to bring in millions of contacts? Or must that be given away for free? When an advertising slogan becomes a company's motto and ends up impacting its strategy, or that company's new product briefs, then maybe the agency should be rewarded some more. When we develop an iPhone app that changes the way a major financial establishment conducts its business, is that something we should be doing for free, too? All these issues can be summed up as a second paradox: "Agencies have never found it so hard to be paid for what they do. Yet advertisers have never needed agencies more than now."

The fact is that several factors have contributed to putting agencies back at the heart of their clients' concerns. First, there is a need for more creativity. The decades-old system based on hammering the same message over and over again is running out of steam. Unless things are catchy, no one notices them. Creativity is no longer just optional.... Secondly, clients require integration, which involves combining every existing discipline, meaning PR, digital, design, merchandising, direct marketing, corporate communication, and advertising. As soon as advertisers come to realize they lack the capacity to combine all these activities, the demands on agencies increase.... Finally, the growing complexity of the media: the Internet has multiplied options exponentially, ideas move differently now. In this context, we have to generate more and more content. Client demand has exploded. One of our Paris agencies makes nearly eight hundred short documentaries a year, usually for the Web. Producing all this material demands new resources. Costly resources.

Like many other businesses, ours is undergoing a major upheaval. Recently, one financial analyst noted that advertising agencies were becoming management consultants, producers of content, business brokers, intellectual property distributors, technology experts, and data analysts. As well as designers of ad campaigns. Right. That's why it certainly looks like advertisers need their agencies more than ever before.

One last point, though. The main duty of an advertising agency is to increase the worth of its client's brands. No one's denying that. Indeed, in the last ten years, brands have increased their share of corporate worth: they now represent the majority of corporations' intangible assets, and these in turn represent more than half of Standard & Poor's 500 companies' aggregate worth. Brand value is now acknowledged as one of companies' biggest assets.

From this observation arises a third paradox: "How can advertising acquire a more central role at a time when companies are more and more skeptical of marketing?" Advertising is nothing more than a marketing tool, so its fate is closely tied to that of marketing. But in many big corporations, marketing is being called into question and criticized. Confidence in marketing is declining. The average length of tenure of marketing directors in the US is twenty-three months. Twenty-three months! Definitely the sign of a beleaguered discipline. Chief executives want their marketing directors to define general strategy, but they don't give them the means to do the job. Misunderstandings and frustration ensue.... How can procurement attach more importance to marketing matters in these circumstances? How can they hold marketing requirements in better regard? How can we explain that marketing is an investment to be optimized, not an expenditure to be minimized?

New Economic Models

John Ruskin was a Victorian art historian and philosopher. He had the good sense to say that when you pay too much for something, all that happens is you lose a little money. When you pay too little for something, sometimes you lose it altogether. What you have bought will no longer be able to perform the function you bought it to perform. Skillful client negotiators would do well to ponder Ruskin's conclusion: "It is unwise to pay too much, but it is worse to pay too little."

The problem agencies are encountering says something about the times we live in. In every field, how to value intangibles is gradually becoming a central issue. The challenges the advertising industry faces are omens other industries should watch because, under postmodern capitalism, most corporate assets will be intangible. People are starting to believe they know how to value brands in financial terms, but assessing intangible capital remains highly perilous; coming up with a figure for wealth that cannot appear on balance sheets, such as human resources, customer base, partnerships, computer systems, total knowledge and skills, image—all things relating to the cognitive economy. Intangibles represent the future both in microeconomic or corporate terms and in macroeconomic or developed economy national terms. Even demand for manufactured goods will rest on the amount of gray matter injected into them. Our ability to define the value of intangible assets, or rather the different valuations of a range of different intangibles, is about to become crucial.

As early as 1994, Esther Dyson, a long-time IT business angel wrote, "The ease with which digital content can be copied and disseminated will eventually force businesses to sell the results of creative activity cheaply, or even give it away. Whatever the product—software, books, music, movies—the cost of creation will have to be recouped indirectly: business will have to distribute intellectual property for free in order to sell services and relationships." This startling prophecy was true enough for a while. Now, things are changing. People are starting to receive compensation for what they do. Apple, for instance, allows compensation for app development. Apple is showing the way. They are paying for creative license and thus proving that Esther Dyson may not be right forever.

The advertising industry needs to find alternative sources of income. In this spirit, our agency is trying to make products that it can sell. Here's an example, one of many: we have designed a piece of mobile phone software for a client that allows people visiting its outlets to access geo-specific digital offers. This software may be adapted and sold to other clients. In other words, we can turn the services we provide into products that we make. The English language offers an endless supply of clumsy but evocative coinages: in this instance, the verb "productize." It means turning something that is not a product into a product.

Yet derivatives like these cannot become the main basis of our remuneration. However profitable, they must be seen for what they are: incremental revenue. Whereas when we organize Disruption Days and Media Arts Days, we are being paid to do our core job. We are being paid for our reason for being. It is important we persevere in this direction.

Advertising is trading in intangibles. Intangibles are moving to the heart of our economies. Many new economic models will be devised. Thousands of imaginative entrepreneurs will invent new ways of monetizing. I don't imagine that cognitive industries, which hold the key to the future of the developed world, can remain undervalued for long. Sooner or later, people will have to learn to value intangibles.

Factory

"We are making stuff." I must say, a response I wasn't expecting.

The location is Media Arts Lab, a part of our LA agency that works exclusively for Apple. For reasons of confidentiality—anything involving Apple has to remain utterly secret—we keep the four hundred staff members involved behind a Chinese wall. There is reinforced security. Staff and guests are fingerprinted on entry. It is a sheltered environment. You can feel the creativity in the air. The future feels physically in the making. As a visitor, every time you pass an employee in the corridor, you feel old. Designers, producers, strategists, writers, visual artists, sociologists, digital wizards, former journalists cross paths here daily. They are looking for ideas. Some of those ideas will impact all of our everyday lives.

To us, the Media Arts Lab is an experiment in the future of our profession. Empirically speaking, it teaches us something every day. Because Apple demands a high level of integration, meaning the ability to bring together, transversally, a variety of disciplines and departments used to working apart. Apple insists that every appearance and mention of the brand should bear the stamp of creativity: it needs to be fresh, innovative, new. Every point of contact between Apple and its customers or potential customers must be treated with utmost care.

James Vincent is one of the rare people who, as Walter Isaacson confirms in his Steve Jobs biography, could speak to Jobs day and night. A year and a half after Media Arts Lab was founded, I asked its president James what had changed. The response came as a surprise. I was expecting to hear how difficult bringing together people of different backgrounds was, about the lack of comprehension between practitioners of different crafts, the divide between digital geeks and the rest, between creative talent and return-on-investment specialists, between media planners and content creators. He said nothing of the kind. What he said was, "We are making stuff." What he meant by this was that bringing all these people together was not just for coming up with ideas, but for actually making things. Making packaging, making websites, making films, apps, newspaper content, events, and expos.... People who work for Media Arts Lab now bring to client meetings finished products or as-good-as-finished products. No PowerPoint presentations, those boring lectures you get when admen listen to the sound of their own voices while screening incomprehensible slides to clients who are longing for concrete ideas.

FACTORY

Making Stuff

When our LA agency was independent, it called itself
"The Idea Factory." It's still that. And now we don't
distinguish between ideas and their realization. We make
no distinction between a project and its execution. We
still manufacture ideas, but we also craft and make things.

We devised and designed the soccer ball for the
2010 World Cup Final in South Africa. This is
something Adidas has been doing on their own since
the 1970 final. This time, they brought in a partner.
We suggested that the Cup's visual grammar, what is
called its graphic charter, as well as the design for the
actual ball, should be based on an idea we baptized
Eleven Threads, eleven threads in eleven different colors
representing the eleven players whose combined
talents drive a team's success. Eleven threads like the
eleven official languages of South Africa spoken by
eleven ethnic groups in a land represented by a single
flag. Eleven threads, eleven languages, eleven players
in support of one another. Our design was not just
elegant. It had meaning.

When I started out in advertising, I never believed
that agencies would end up making so many actual
things. Back then we designed films and posters. Now
we build websites, too. We invent packaging. We devise
content. We produce events.

For Nissan, we created Qashqai Car Games out
of Europe. A road surface morphed into a giant

skateboard track. Instead of people on rollerblades, we had SUVs. We put videos on the Net showing experienced race-car drivers performing impressive virtual stunts, spinning through the air at the wheel of their cars. During the first season, these videos were seen fourteen million times. The following season, they were seen twenty-two million times. A Qashqai Car Games website had pilot interviews and Internet user comments. The word "Qashqai" became a generic term for crossover vehicles all over Europe.

In 2005, we launched the Pedigree Adoption Drive to encourage the adoption of stray dogs and shelter funding. We broadcast films on TV, published a guide to adopting dogs, built a store in Times Square in New York so people could find a dog and take it home there and then. Millions of dollars have been raised. Thousands of dogs have been adopted. The dogs we show on TV generally find an owner that same day. It's hard saying no to a dog that looks straight into the camera and says (in voice-over), "The more time passes, the more my chances decrease."

The Qashqai Car Games lasted two seasons. The Pedigree Adoption Drive has been going for six years. We also participated in one-off events, including two of the most famous events in entertainment, the Grammy Awards and the Oscars. We made thirty-second videos for the Grammys recapping every nominated artist's career. We designed a tool known as the Fan Buzz Visualizer that measures artists' popularity by going through the Internet with a fine-tooth comb and collecting every single reference to an artist. Not surprisingly, Lady Gaga was the most popular artist in 2010.

For the Oscars, we devised a campaign based on famous lines in Hollywood movies, like "I'm king of the world," spoken by Leonardo DiCaprio in *Titanic* or "You talking to me?" a Robert de Niro line in *Taxi Driver*. Seventy-five quotes in all, selected from nominated feature films between 1936 and 2005, were used in a poster campaign, the Oscars Web site, and Spike Lee's commercials. These are the lines movie fans don't want to forget. They belong to American culture.

More recently, we killed Justin Timberlake, Serena Williams, Alicia Keys, and other stars to raise funds to fight AIDS. The campaign said: "Justin Timberlake is dead," "Serena Williams is dead".... This was only virtual murder, of course. No more Facebook, no more Twitter, no more messages to fans on blogs, no more gossip on the Internet.... In order to bring their favorite stars back to life, we told fans they had to pay a digital ransom of ten dollars each. A few days later, the funds needed were raised and fans could bring their stars back to life again...on the Internet. The campaign had temporarily sacrificed virtual lives to save real lives.

Reality Effect

These examples build a connection between real life and its virtual extension on the Net. In fact, over the last few years, the actual meaning of the word "virtual" has been transformed. Today, virtual means what exists, but online. Real means what happens in real life, in other words, off-line. On TV, for example. But it wasn't always this way. TV commercials describe a world that seems closed and enchanted and artificial, detached from people's everyday reality. That's why, before the Internet, commercials were often described as being larger than life, almost "virtual."

It was always my aim to make reality penetrate the artificial world of advertising. Over the years, I often used to quote Chevys, the California restaurant chain that serves only fresh, non-frozen food, as an example. To underline what makes Chevys different, Goodby Silverstein, its agency, produced a very large number of cheap and therefore disposable commercials that could be trashed the same day, after airing. The message was spelled in large font at the end of each spot: "Fresh TV." The commercials were fresh. So was the product. A concrete production idea made the message much stronger. The reality effect disrupted perception. Suddenly, reality penetrated into the closeted world of advertising commercials. Fresh TV gave you something to remember. It gave your memory something solid to grab hold of.

In the early nineties, we advised Danone to set up a giant boutique in the center of Paris, to install dozens of serially connected TVs, like computer screens in financial market trading rooms. Visitors would have access to the best documentary movies in the world on the connection between food and health. Though we didn't know it, what we were suggesting was actually a proto-Web site. A kind of real-life Web site....

Around the same time, I was reminding Club Med management you couldn't tell people all there was to know about Club Med in a thirty-second spot. Not by far. So I suggested producing a thirty-minute documentary about all that Club Med "villages" had to offer. Then making a thirty-second commercial to launch the documentary. The ad would be about how important it is for a father not to miss his annual week's vacation with his wife and kids. We were going to use the ad to tell that dad to go out and buy the documentary before he made the booking, to make sure he ended up in the right place. Again, we were trying to achieve what today's websites can do, namely, by providing as much useful information as possible. Both times, in the case of Danone and in the case of Club Med, what was important was making the message practical and tangible. Injecting reality.

Nothing is more practical than an Apple app. They bring the virtual reality of the Internet into real life. There are hundreds of thousands of such apps now, many offering useful services. They are such a success that Steve Jobs liked to categorize two decades of recent computer history into three periods: PCs, with Microsoft; the Internet, with Google; and apps, with Apple.

Not long ago, we developed an app for Club Med that does more than we ever imagined might be possible twenty years ago. Soon, you'll be able to visit every "village" using an iPhone. You'll be able to enter a Club Med village, check in at reception, walk through the grounds, visit rooms. All using a handheld iPhone or iPad. And when you retrace your steps, the image will spin around 360 degrees. Every single detail will be visible. The reality of a "village'" located some ten thousand miles away will be at your fingertips.

Since we work for Apple ourselves, developing as many iPad/iPhone apps as we can is only natural. One helps smokers give up. As soon as they want to light a cigarette, friends dissuade them in real time on their phones. *Music Mapper* relates places to songs anywhere in the world. First kiss? Marriage proposal? They're often identified with a particular tune. *The Iconist* collects striking recent photographs in the world of luxury. *Re-View* provides real-time insider access to global breaking financial news. *Semi-Precious* offers new design reviews. *Nivea Sun* assesses the sun-block you need according to age, skin-type, and location. *British Airways by British Airways* allows you to download boarding passes onto your iPhone and also proposes last-minute upgrades. In Japan, the *Giants Digital Tryout* app helps baseball fans assess their pitching, batting, running, and catching abilities. The best get to use the app to test themselves against professional Tokyo team players, and to meet them. Last but not least, *Drinkspiration* by Absolut offers you a choice of some four hundred cocktail recipes, arranged according to the taste you're looking for, the colors you prefer, the weather outside, the time of day, and the bar you're in....

Three hundred and sixty-five days a year, our network launches new apps. Apps extend brands limitlessly. They enrich their content.

Brand Content

Our industry has changed at breakneck speed. We are making all kinds of content now. Our agencies are constantly generating documentaries, short features, Web episodes, mobile phone videos, and so on. For example, we made a series of movies for Visa during the Vancouver Winter Olympics. These were portraits of sports champions, such as US Olympic medalist Julia Mancuso. During the Games, a digital link gave web users access to athletes' anxiety and tension immediately prior to competing. The fact that major athletes gave us access to film them in real time just a few seconds before and after an event truly enhanced these pieces' authentic worth.

Perhaps the most spectacular editorial content "manufactured" by our agency concerns Gatorade. This was such a success that CNN ranked it among its top stories. Fox Sports bought the rights. Now we're into our fourth season.

Separated by the Delaware River, Easton, PA, and Phillipsburg, NJ, have had a deep-rooted history in football rivalry since 1906. Every Thanksgiving for more than one hundred years, the two teams have competed for a trophy known as the "Fork of the Delaware." In 1993, a hard-fought game ended in a

91

frustrating 7–7 tie. Sixteen years later, we ran the same game again, with the same players, coached by the same coaches, refereed by the same referees, cheered by the same cheerleaders. For three months, these aging players went back into training. They lost weight. They gave it all they had. They drank Gatorade. Film crews filmed them. Web users watched them get back into shape. Day by day. Ounce by ounce.

On April 25, 2009, the reenacted game was played in a packed, twenty-thousand-seat stadium. Tickets sold out over the Internet within ninety minutes, some at a very high markup. More than three hundred cable stations provided coverage. A few months later, Fox Sports adopted the idea of replaying old matches, sponsored by Gatorade. In the second season, we had a hockey game, in the third, a baseball game.... *Contagious*, the advertising professional's bible, said, "Many brands have generated quality content over the past few years, but Gatorade's program is unique in that it has created a real event. With huge ratings." Once again, reality heightens impact.

We have entered into an era when editorial teams are increasingly anxious to make news programs entertaining. Every moment has to be spectacular. Watch CNN for just a few moments: see how the barrier that separates information from entertainment has diminished. Major events that justify repeated news updates are given names like serials: "Desert Storm," "The Arab Spring," "Angry Planet." Audiences follow developments day by day like episodes unfolding in the plot of a soap opera. Correspondingly, companies like Chevys and Gatorade have copied the way media behave, calling their campaigns "Fresh TV" or "Replay." We no longer just write slogans to cap thirty-second commercials. We name the events we devise with headline-grabbing titles like you see on TV. Thus Qashqai Car Games, Absolut Hunk, Pedigree Adoption Drive, Skittles Rainbow Experience, and MTV's Day of No Design.

Life is different now. Brands have become publishers. But one thing remains unchanged: the quality of the writing makes the difference. We keep hunting for the right word, the most skillfully crafted phrase. Our profession has inspired some wonderful pieces of writing and many striking titles. Advertising anthologies are packed with them. When we make movies, when we build websites, when we produce short programs, we must maintain a respect for good writing, a love of craft well done. Many people see our business as an industry. It must remain a craft.

Global

On May 22nd, 1981, just over thirty years ago, President François Mitterrand of France created a new government department. He called it the "Ministry for Leisure Time."

In light of today's high unemployment, economic fears, and crises, this may sound weird. Was Mitterrand a utopian? Or was he just plain blind? But back then, the world was meant to be entering a new Age of Leisure. At the time, everyone—in France at least—thought this was a grand idea. Western countries had just experienced three decades of solid growth. There was no reason to think things would change. Future generations' standards of living must inexorably rise. Increasing productivity would inevitably reduce working hours. So we needed a government ministry, since in an over-centralized country like mine the State wants to poke its nose into everything. Even the time we spend not working.

Europe Left Behind

Thirty years later, Chinese people, Indians, Brazilians work a great deal more than we do. And even though France has one of the highest hourly productivity rates in the world, we work an insufficient number of hours. My country is becoming less competitive by the day compared with emerging nations. Successive governments have fallen prey to illusion. France is now out of sync with the rest of the world. Joseph Stiglitz, Nobel Prize winner in Economics, puts it this way: "If we fail to embrace change, the risk is that we will become a rich country inhabited by poor people."

The sad thing is that until recently, France still held a number of strong cards. Its GNP was the fifth highest in the world. It ranked fourth in terms of exports. Its economy was flourishing. And many of its achievements were scarcely known. It was, for example, the world's number-one exporter of digital services per capita. Even now, it has plenty of powerful cards in its hand. Of the five hundred top companies in the world, thirty-nine are French. Interbrand ranks France fourth in terms of the accumulated value of its major international brands. And Millward Brown considers that, out of the ten brands with the highest momentum, four are French.

But back to the Ministry for Leisure Time. Things started to decline around 1983. Suddenly, the unemployment curve turned upward. The Ministry was abolished.

96

France is a medium-sized power. It can only progress if Europe as a whole progresses. And in many ways, Europe has what it takes. It has no major external imbalance. It produces more than any other region in the world, and in less time and with less energy. The euro has enabled it to make the most of its internal market, the world's largest. But Europe has for a long time now seemed abashed, divided, adrift, even more so with the current financial crisis.

To people of my generation, it seems like Europe is the great missed opportunity. A giant historical error was made in 1973. Haunted by traditional anti-German demons, the then French president, Georges Pompidou, did all he could to speed up Britain's joining The European Union. He hoped Britain would offer a counterweight to German influence. But Europe's Founding Fathers had designed Europe in 1957 around a nucleus of six countries. Their idea was that there should be a gradual process, first of economic federation, and then of political union. Britain saw what was then known as the European Community as a free trade area and nothing more. For over forty years now, it has done nothing other than hinder fiscal, social, and political union.

A better route would have been to encourage the original six countries to move more rapidly toward union through the seventies and eighties. And to force future candidates to modify their institutions and to improve their social and economic policies in order to meet much stricter entry criteria.... Subsequent enlargement has proceeded at an uncontrolled pace.

Hardly anyone in Europe today knows how many countries are in the Union. The answer is twenty-seven. And every important decision must be taken on a basis of unanimity. I've got nothing against Slovakia, but late last year Slovakia blocked financial aid to Greece for a period of several weeks, putting the entire world in danger of financial meltdown. I do not believe this is the Europe the Founding Fathers dreamed of in the fifties, a vision later reinforced through the profound friendship between Charles De Gaulle and Konrad Adenauer.

We have wasted decades. Yet never was time so precious. The only—inadequate—response to the sovereign debt crisis, acceptable to both Germany and France, is to amend the European Treaty. This could take months, even years, since it is not easy for small countries to agree to abandon the unanimity rule they cherish. So changing the Treaty is a long-term prospect unrelated to the urgency of solutions needed. Europe has yet to notice that time is not on its side.

Meanwhile, in the rest of the world, everything seems to be moving faster and faster. The BRICs are facing competition from what are now known as the Next Eleven, a group that includes such countries as South Korea, Nigeria, Mexico, South Africa, Vietnam, and Indonesia. In the past, people in Europe failed to grasp just how far globalization would extend and what was at stake. Now, they understand globalization, but they're still underestimating its speed. Europe is dithering.

98

Unbridled Acceleration

Contrary to prevailing wisdom on the global village during the eighties, globalization is not standardizing and unifying the world as much as people say. In reality, it englobes a series of contradictory trends, fragile equilibriums, disproportionate risks, and obscure threats, making them appear universal. People are astonished and stunned at what the future seems to hold. We feel that we are losing our ability to understand and control. Philosopher Pierre Manent says, "The spirit has lost confidence in itself." Countries such as ours that always took pride in their supposed superior capacity for understanding feel especially at a loss. The quickening pace of globalization is being imposed upon us. We have no choice about that. As to the current recession, it relates to a deeper, more entrenched trend, an unprecedented crisis, although predicted as early as 1918 by Oswald Spengler in his *Decline of the West*. With brutal clarity, a new geopolitical reality is emerging. The world has reached a turning point.

An interview with the CEO of South Korea's Samsung electronics company in *Le Figaro* newspaper gives an indication of future East Asian economic growth. Question: "Your revenue stands at one hundred billion euros per year. What will it be in 2020?" Answer: "Four hundred billion euros."

One hundred fifty billion euros, even two hundred billion euros might have sounded about right....

Doubling revenue in a decade would be pretty good for any industrial company. But quadrupling it? Samsung may or may not attain its objective. The crucial fact is that Asian chairmen are giving themselves goals way above those set by Western executives. Some will succeed, others won't. Those that do will bring a whole cohort of fellow national subcontractors in their wake—not to mention competitors.

Another example. BYD is a Chinese company that makes batteries for phones. It has attained world leadership within just a few years, a 30 percent market share. Its CEO has decided to diversify and create a vertically integrated company. As a maker of lithium batteries, he has chosen to invest massively in electric engines. His plan is first that BYD will be the leader in electric cars in China as early as 2015. Then the largest carmaker by 2020. And with one success leading to the next, the world leader in the car industry by 2025. Will he make it? Maybe not. Still, as of now, every big player in car manufacturing is impressed by BYD. And Warren Buffet has taken a 10 percent stake in the company.

Everything in China moves faster. While we're on automobiles, China is already the largest market for cars on the planet. More cars were sold in Greater Beijing in 2010 than in the entire United Kingdom. Chinese authorities have launched a giant project called "The Clean Car Project." The idea is to produce some five million electric cars in China by 2020. This will make China world leader in this new industry. By a very wide margin.

Big Asian companies are not just planning products of the future. They are snapping up Western companies, too. Since Lenovo bought IBM's PC business and Tata purchased Jaguar and Land Rover, it has been clear that Asian companies are out to conquer the world. Soon we will being seeing not just South-North buyouts, but also South-South activity on a giant scale, gigantic mergers and acquisitions that have nothing to do with big Western or big Japanese groups.... Indian and Chinese companies will no longer be targeting sales only to middle-class customers in Asia or South America. They will be making high added-value goods to compete with Western firms, at highly competitive prices. Their goods will attract Western customers as Western purchasing power stagnates or declines. They are knocking at the door of our international advertising networks to learn how to conquer the world by selling their *Created in China* (and not just *Made in China*) products.

The year 2010 was a landmark in the history of China. This was the year China took second place from Japan in the world economic power rankings. Since the days of Deng Xiaoping's ideological U-turn, the Chinese economy has increased a hundredfold. Four of the top ten stock market capitalization firms are now Chinese.

"They will get old before they get rich"—a snappy *Economist* headline sums up the question marks over China's future. Competing with the US is all very well, but winning that contest will require establishing a stable social system. China's failure to open up is going to make things increasingly problematic. China's issues are as big as the country itself. Chinese people are allowed only one child each, so there won't be enough money for pensions. Wages are still much lower in China than in neighboring Japan. The growth of recent decades has been the result of a massive export policy. This is now going to have to give way, partially at least, to a rise in internal demand...China is really two countries. In major cities, standards of living are gradually reaching Western levels; everywhere else they are failing to keep pace. Keith Smith, the head of our international operations, recently told me, "You really need to think of China as Europe and Africa combined."

Despite this, Pricewaterhouse forecasts that if China overcomes the obstacles in its path, its GNP will overtake that of the US in around 2030. It will do this if it manages to accelerate its internal-demand growth rate. And if instead of just copying Western technology, China is starting to generate inventions of its own. On this score, however, China is not lagging as far behind as people think. Just the opposite. The statistical institute Eurostat analyzes every country's share in the worldwide export of high technology. It may come as a surprise to learn that in this domain China has already overtaken Japan, as early as 2003, Europe in 2006, and the United States in 2007.

China is already the world's premier industrial power. The world's premier exporter. The world's premier consumer of energy. Its labs and its companies register more patents than any other country's. It is home to more researchers and engineers than anywhere else. More companies were floated on the Hong Kong and Shanghai stock exchanges in 2011 than in London and New York combined. The list of domains in which China comes first is endless. Even in unexpected sectors, such as art auction houses: an auction house in Hong Kong now does more business than Christie's or Sotheby's.

This may seem like a rapid breakthrough. Actually, it's more of a comeback. At the end of the nineteenth century, China's economy was twice as large as Japan's. Similarly—though this always surprises some people— South America's economy was the same size as North America's. Catching up will bring about a renaissance. The word "renaissance," as used to describe fifteenth-century Europe, applies to what is going on in Asia today. Globalization is allowing countries whose culture suffered a setback during the colonial period to get back on track. This will involve rediscovering their past and also projecting into the future, to lay the foundations for the new civilization to come. The Chinese think of themselves as having created the greatest civilization the world has ever known. The Middle Empire, as it was once called, no longer wants to be just in the middle. China sees itself as an ever-increasing circle, gradually expanding to encompass the rest of the world.

India will soon be competing with China. If it can accelerate its speed of change. Average growth in India is around 7 percent. This may sound like a lot to us anemic Westerners, but it is still not enough. According to the Indian government, India needs double-digit growth if it is to start reducing the poverty levels of its poorest inhabitants.

Just as there as are two Chinas, there are two Indias. There are more or less privileged regions and categories of population. But, unlike in China, the fault line between the two Indias takes the form of an opposition between conservatives and modernists.

Most of the inhabitants seem closed to the outside world. At the same time, Indian companies are conquering the globe. Mittal won a hostile takeover battle against Arcelor. Tata has launched the cheapest car ever made. Infosys is winning market share every day against Western leaders in the IT sector. Bangalore is in many ways emerging as a threat to Silicon Valley. Globalization has brought the Indian economy undreamt-of opportunities. However, many people within India are criticizing this strategy of global conquest. Commentators and other establishment figures are arguing in favor of isolationism. Indian values, they say, are eternal. The rest of the world is degrading.

The *Financial Times India* has reacted by launching a campaign in praise of openness and economic growth. This campaign is entitled *The Time Is Now*. It calls on famous Bollywood stars as spokespersons. Amitabh Bachchan is one. He gives a moving two-minute speech in the manner of Rudyard Kipling, a forty-line ode to India. He is seen saying, "One India lies in the optimism of our hearts. The other India looks in the skepticism of our minds." He speaks of the new, vibrant, and dynamic India on the rise. An India more intent on success than enslaved to a fear of failure. He explains that India no longer boycotts foreign-made products. Instead, it buys the companies that make them. He remarks that history never warns us when it has reached a turning point. And he concludes, "This is that rarely ever moment. History is turning a page."

You have to see Amitabh Bachchan delivering this speech in an improbable combination of styles, from whisper to harangue. He knows India is on the road to success. And this self-confidence actually multiplies the chances of success exponentially.

Cultural Dialogue

What about Africa?... Half the population of Africa still lives beneath the poverty threshold. Yet this continent that once seemed so hopeless is now steadily joining the concert of nations. Many of Africa's statistical indicators, many of its ratios and indices, are now at last taking a turn for the better. From the early days of the postcolonial era onward, everything seemed to go from bad to worse. The independence years were hard enough, but the decades from 1980 to 2000 proved catastrophic. The images of Africa we carry in our heads date back to that period. The preconceived ideas and prejudices, too. Few people know that since the year 2000, economic growth in Africa has been running at twice its population growth. This means the population figures are no longer a handicap but an

105

unexpected strength: Africa is an empty place with low population density.

So says Lionel Zinsou, whom I heard give a talk about the tipping point in Africa. Lionel Zinsou is a part-French, part-Beninois investment banker with a senior doctorate in economics. For a time, he managed a division at Danone, the French multinational. His analysis is that Africa is on the brink of radical change, as evidenced by GNP, which has tripled over the last eight years. Zinsou says Africa is going to become a new workshop for the world, following in China and India's footsteps. He emphasizes a little-known fact, an encouraging trend in financial statistics. Inflation in Africa is now down to almost nothing. Local currencies are strengthening. Government budgets are generating surpluses. One consequence is that nearly five hundred billion dollars worth of foreign currency reserves have piled up in the strongboxes of African central banks, representing some 43 percent of GNP. In just six years, Africa has repaid its debt. No other continent has ever performed such a feat. A continent without debt is a free continent.

One task, though, remains. African countries need to regain an identity; they need to restore their culture and rid themselves of the showy crassness born of the ruling classes' habit of siphoning public funds. Ousmane Sow is Africa's best-known sculptor. He has shown at the Guggenheim in New York. He was the person who employed the term "showy crassness" in front of me. My wife is a sculptor. A painter grasps light. A sculptor captures motion. Ousmane Sow sees that gift in Marie-Virginie's work. From time to time, we meet. Last time we were in Dakar, Ousmane told us a story that saddened him. The president of Senegal, Abdoulaye Wade, has erected a monument to the glory of the African Renaissance on a promontory off the coast of Dakar. It is one hundred feet high. It shows a man, a woman, and a child staring out over the horizon, in a composition that only old-style Communist leaders can appreciate. It is a work of almost perfect hideousness.

Ousmane Sow had suggested an alternative project, a tunnel jutting from out of the Atlantic Ocean, from which dozens of clay figures, carved and modeled in his inimitable style, would have emerged, representing a population of slaves returning home from America to the land of their heritage. Much more meaningful. Much more beautiful. He also proposed that a parallel tunnel should be built on the East Coast of the US. The tunnel would plunge into the ocean, only this time the single file of slaves would not be emerging from the tunnel, but entering it. The two spectacular monuments on either side of the Atlantic Ocean would in actual fact be a single monument: the first transatlantic sculpture. A symbol of Africa's rebirth, sponsored by America. We miss this work of art. Now that it already exists in one man's mind, it leaves a gap in our virtual global museum.

Ousmane Sow's career as a sculptor began in the days when Senegal's president was Leopold Senghor, one of the most open-minded spirits on the planet. A "citizen of the world" before the expression was coined. He was a graduate of France's most prestigious literature and philosophy university. He was probably one of the most civilized and best-educated statesmen ever to have been elected. As early as 1977, he laid out his vision for what the encounter of civilizations, the meeting of nations—globalization—might bring, if only it could be not just a by-product of the market but a catalyst toward a new humanism. Senghor listed a number of instances of convergence. I remember one in particular, which was an analysis of the affinities between Japanese and African verse. He pointed out that Senegalese poetry and Japanese haikus have a similar minimal aesthetic. He shared his perception with the Japanese ambassador in Dakar. Unbelievably, the Japanese embassy set about organizing haiku competitions in Senegal.

The title of Leopold Senghor's best-known work sounds like a prayer at the dawning of a globalized world. It was called *Dialogue Between Cultures*.

Hostile Takeover

Hawk Strike and Swift Bite were two companies BDDP came to own for a while.

BDDP was the advertising company we founded in 1984 in Paris, with the ambition of building a global network. In 1989, we wrote a new chapter in the episode of the Hundred Years' War that set France against Britain six centuries ago. We launched a hostile takeover bid for BMP, one of the leading advertising firms in Britain. "Bold but stupid," trumpeted the commentators. The best executives would leave the firm, they said, if our bid succeeded, and take their clients with them. The received wisdom was that there was no such thing as a successful hostile takeover bid against a service company.

But there is one way to pull such a bid off. The trick is to turn opinion inside the firm under siege around within the first few weeks, transforming a hostile takeover bid into a friendly one. This was our aim. Martin Sorrell at WPP had already paved the way. Hearing that Ogilvy & Mather, the venerable agency he had established thirty years earlier, was in danger of losing its independence to WPP, David Ogilvy called Martin Sorrell "an odious personage." Nonetheless, a few weeks later David Ogilvy allowed himself to be appointed chairman of the new combined outfit.... But were the British going to accept the French doing to them what they had done to the Americans?

Frog Off

British advertising was bursting with creativity. One English reporter even had the nerve to call London the "Athens of advertising." Ridley Scott, Hugh Hudson, and Alan Parker were the kings of the British commercials scene. And BMP was one of the most brilliant agencies there. We had several meetings with them, convinced a merger between our two groups would be bound to establish one of the best international networks. BMP had a minority in the best-regarded agency in San Francisco, run by Jeff Goodby. It owned one of the most creative agencies in New York, which shared the BMW account with us. On paper, the match made sense. But, predictably, neither BMP nor we would agree to relinquish control in a combined venture. Still, despite this, we were certain the idea made sense. We decided to launch a takeover bid, which, under the circumstances, could only be considered hostile.

The rules stipulate that there must be a forty-day period between opening and closing a bid. Whatever the outcome, this is always a time of outright warfare.

We made some blunders. One was omitting to check the names of the shell companies we had to buy in order to launch the bid. Under British law, takeover rules stipulate a buyer can purchase up to 4.99 percent of a company's shares on the open market without having to declare its intent. But the rumor mill always cranks into action. People end up finding out who is out there buying. Which is why, in order to stay anonymous as long as possible, a purchaser uses shell companies (companies that already exist but have no real business activity) to go into action. We bought two of them. They duly went in and snapped up BMP stock. Everything was moving really fast. Our lawyers neglected to tell us what these shell companies were called. Then, two months later, as the bid process was in full swing, we found out. They were called "Hawk Strike" and "Swift Bite." The reporters, the market, and above all the directors of BMP all found out at the same time we did. Just when we were trying to convince them our intentions were friendly.

How in all decency could frog-eating Frenchmen gobble up an English firm? The response was a deadly "Frog off!"

In the UK, it was normal practice to insult your adversaries during a takeover bid. A radio ad was broadcast that called us straw Napoleons whose breath reeked of garlic and liquor. We were asked to attend a secret meeting—attackers and defenders are not supposed to meet—in a basement at a BMP subsidiary's office. Ten BMP bosses sat in a semicircle. They asked us to take a seat. They said, "Withdraw."

111

Then they got up and left. John Webster was probably the best copywriter British advertising has ever known. To this day, I remember the haughty look he gave us as he left the room.

We persisted. Weeks went by. Hostile reports in the British press subsided. Here and there, favorable pieces on our group started appearing, as well as commentary confirming the strategic soundness of our approach. Later, the *Financial Times* went so far as to praise our "small advertising group with big ambitions." Then, a few days before the fateful end of the forty-day period, just when we were about to win, a white knight appeared, flying to the rescue of our British "victims." That was it. We lost to Omnicom.

A Frenchman in the US

It was at this time that Mary Wells, sitting in New York, first heard of us. Her agency, Wells Rich Greene, had come out of the creative revolution started by Bill Bernbach in the sixties. It had expanded enormously over the years and at that time employed a staff of five hundred, ranking third in the New York agency listings by size. A year later, we bought Mary Wells's company, accumulating huge debt as we did so. Buying it would give us a place on the world stage. It would also pave the way to winning major international clients.

Things turned out very differently. We were unable to service the disproportionate debt we had taken on.

Acquiring Wells thus put an end to our adventures at BDDP. We lost everything we had, or nearly.

Then in 1998, BDDP was fortunate to join Omnicom and then merged with TBWA. Omnicom is run by John Wren. Unlike his more adventurous rivals at other major holding companies, he has always preferred internal to external growth. And wisely so. His group's performance is all the more solid for that. But it hasn't stopped him from making a few carefully chosen strategic acquisitions.

It is a twist of fate that BDDP has contributed, until recently, more than any other agency to Omnicom's external growth. The two big operations we were involved in, our failed takeover bid against BMP and our acquisition of Wells, have turned out to be very beneficial to Omnicom. Following our hostile bid, Omnicom, as I have said, was able to take in one of Britain's market leaders, BMP, as well as its San Francisco agency, one of the best in the world. Next, following the confusion caused by our acquisition of Wells, Omnicom could merge BDDP with TBWA, the junior of Omnicom's three networks at the time, thus giving TBWA the critical mass it lacked.

A consequence of these episodes was that, within a few years, I was put in charge of TBWA. Running an American group is a challenge for any French person. People from the English-speaking world dominate the advertising sector. I may be an experienced professional, but I still have occasion to feel uneasy. I feel, somehow, that I have entered a world that is not mine.

We are wrong in thinking that because we both belong to the Western world, American and European cultures are close. On the surface, many attitudes do seem to match. But beneath the surface, they remain very different. As Felix Rohatyn, former US ambassador to France, once said, "I thought we shared the same culture and that our interests diverged. In fact, the opposite is true. Our interests are the same and our cultures are quite apart."

Joint Venture

A few years ago, I met an Asian politician who has always felt at ease with US business culture. We discussed hostile takeovers. He ran his country, he said, according to corporate methods of governance in the US. His name is Lee Kuan Yew, Singapore's founding father.

When Lee Kuan Yew made his painful break with Malaysia, he found himself in charge of a city without a future. The rest of the story is well known. In just two generations, he made an astonishing success of Singapore, now one of the world's best-regarded capital cities. *From Third World to First* is the title of one of Lee Kuan Yew's books. Forty-six years of authoritarian paternalism have given the citizens of Singapore, the tiny Southeast Asian island state, one of the highest standards of living in the world. It is hardly surprising that it was after a trip to Singapore that Deng Xiaoping decided, in 1978, to ordain China's great change.

Lee Kuan Yew ran Singapore with an iron fist, and as if it were a private corporation. When I was asked to interview him, in the spring of 2009, we discussed the parallels between running a country and running a company. My first question was, "In what sense is Singapore a brand?"

This interview capped the first "World Effies", an advertising festival designed to award the most effective campaigns. The managers of the Effies had insisted that the event should take place somewhere other than New York. They chose Singapore. The city played host to representatives from the worldwide advertising business. Two days of speeches and celebrations were organized. Lee Kuan Yew was asked to participate. The interview before an audience of one thousand people was to be the highlight of the week: the closing event. I knew that the former prime minister was respected, but I did not realize quite how far the worship went. The ovation he received when he entered the hall was gripping. Then came the succession of questions and answers. Despite his eighty years of age, the mind of the "Minister Mentor"—such is his official title – is still sharp.

One question came into my mind that was not on the list he had been sent in advance. It was a question he might find incongruous, even impertinent. "Minister Mentor, you have just spent one hour comparing your country to a corporation. We have discussed its exceptional growth. But as you know, companies expand in two ways, internally and externally. If you could buy another country, which would you choose?"

Silence. The audience was embarrassed. After a moment's hesitation, Lee Kuan Yew consented to an answer. His eyes twinkled. The audience relaxed. He gave a list of potential candidates, starting with Malaysia, commenting, however, that the history of Singapore's painful birth through partition meant that he didn't see his Malaysian neighbors agreeing to a purchase. He spoke of the Philippines, much too chaotic for his well-known orderly tastes. He ran through all the states in Indochina. I don't recall every one of his comments. I was focusing on the next questions. He touched on Thailand, the only country in the region to have succeeded in preserving its independence. Which made an agreed takeover improbable. And so forth.

"The ideal country would be a country with a bit of space. We are too tightly packed here in Singapore. It must be a country that, from an economic point of view, has passed a tipping point and is starting to make progress. We are better at speeding things up than correcting them," he added. "And as you know, people think of me as authoritarian. So I don't think a hostile takeover would work. Rather than a takeover, I should prefer a joint venture. That's it. I think we should offer Vietnam a joint venture."

He smiled, certain of his effect, and we returned to the more conventional subject matter of our talk. Lee Kuan Yew is right. Hostile takeovers, in the services industry at least, rarely work out. Either the aggressor is foiled by a white knight and the operation fails, or his attack succeeds, and he finds himself faced with an impossible task of his own making: having to make a success of a forced marriage between a wounded company and a company whose culture is seen as bellicose. The only thing that is certain is that, one way or another, the company under attack will lose its independence. As soon as a takeover is launched, people in the company know their board is going to be turned upside down. And that the future will not hold what its managers, often its founders, had planned.

Martin Boase was the B in BMP. Years after our hostile bid, I asked him to lunch in London to make some sort of amends. In hindsight, I realized that what we put one of the crown jewels of the world advertising business through was unforgivable. Raiders do things like that. We should not have. It was a sin against the spirit.

Barely had Martin sat down when he suggested we steer clear of the subject of our bid. We chatted about this and that. I can picture him now, the very essence of gentlemanly self-control. Through all our battles, he never lost his natural elegance. As the English say, "Class is grace under pressure."

Ideas

"An idea is something people have an active desire to remember."

This was said by Philippe Michel, who had been BBDO's chief executive in France for two decades. To this day, he remains the most influential creative talent in French advertising. I've adopted Philippe's aphorism as my own. I like the intrusion of desire into memory. Desire for a brand and desire to remember ideas often go hand in hand. The former is the fruit of the latter.

Brands and ideas are inseparable. A brand that comes with no idea attached is a brand that has been deactivated. Brands are judged and appreciated as much for the ideas they inspire as for the goods and services they offer. They're expected to "sponsor" ideas.

Three of my colleagues have written books about ideas. Philippe Michel, in a book published posthumously, asks a question which provides him with his title, *What's the Idea?* His approach is what you might call anthropological. In *The Killer Idea*, Nicolas Bordas, president of TBWA France, offers a semiotic analysis of the notion. And John Hunt, our network's worldwide creative director, who has written many successful books and plays in his native South Africa, focuses on the psychology of creative people and the psychology of those who buy their ideas, namely advertisers. His book is called *The Art of the Idea.*

All three have one thing in common. Their authors start off talking about "the idea" as an advertising concept and go on to discuss "the idea" as a thing in its own right. According to them, the ideas we come up with to promote brands, commercial ideas, give us insight into all sorts of other ideas, however configured. The world of advertising and communication is a field in which to study how ideas are born and how they disseminate. Advertising is raw material. It offers an example with which to judge the world of ideas in general.

The parallel only works up to a certain point, but it is inspiring nonetheless. It provokes some nicely expressed thoughts like this one, from Nicolas Bordas: "All too often, we look at ideas the way we look at snapshots. We ought to be looking at them the way we look at movies. They have a beginning, a middle and an end. The strength of an idea can be assessed in terms of its dynamism; in terms of the trace it leaves." John Hunt says, "Most big ideas started out as fragile little things." And Philippe Michel adds, "Ideas make the world, not the other way round."

Advertising ideas. Marketing ideas. Campaign ideas. Pretty soon, you start thinking our business overuses the word "idea." You begin to think people in advertising have broken into the non-commercial world, stolen the word "idea," and perverted its meaning. But there is no other word to describe what we do. We come up with ideas. We're always on the lookout for ideas that will give our brands a head start. This is a matter of life and death to us. The growth in messages screaming for our attention is so exponential, it creates a planetary hubbub. Very few things surface above the fray. For ages, advertisers thought all they had to do was to repeat conventional messages over and over again. Sooner or later people would hear what they had to say. For weeks on end, advertising campaigns ran like repeated soliloquies. Well, those days are gone. People are immune to such tactics. The Internet offers innumerable escape routes. There is only one way now: providing brands with ideas that are so strong that their customers will actively want to adopt them.

Brand Ideas

The notion of ideas in advertising really took off with the advent of TV advertising. Before that, in the days of print, copywriters ruled. They were judged by the quality of their slogans and headlines, the same way a journalist was judged on the impact of his front page. As soon as someone wrote the slogan, it was rushed down into the studio, where a layout artist would set it. The copywriter never saw his work again, except on the printed page. The slogans were rarely based on an idea. The power was in the writing. There was usually a pun, an alliteration, a paradox of some sort. If the ad actually contained an idea, this was accidental. Only the words mattered. Images (the visuals, as we call them) were there as illustration. Period.

Then TV happened. There was a premium on brevity. The skill became to get a message across in limited time. Thirty-second spots replaced the printed page. Time, not space, was what mattered. The best copywriters were under the illusion that magazine readers used to dawdle over their ads. I'm not so sure. In any case, a TV audience couldn't stop over a good ad. It had to be based on a strong idea, an idea that struck the imagination. "An arresting idea," as we say.

So advertising ideas as we now know them were born with TV. They have evolved over time. They have taken on a range of different forms. I divide this evolution into three stages. In the beginning, people in advertising were only looking for film ideas: to prove that a saucepan was heat-resistant at high temperatures, you showed two saucepans on a gas ring, one inside another. The rival saucepan, the one inside, melted. The demonstration was beyond appeal. The commercial stuck in the mind. But you couldn't spin off other commercials from it. By which I mean that it contained no other idea bigger than itself. It was what our profession calls a "one-shot." Most of the TV commercials of the seventies fall into this category. Next came the notion of a TV campaign. A big idea inspires a whole series of different commercials. I remember "The Most Misunderstood Soft Drink" for

Dr. Pepper, "Everything You Always Wanted From a Beer. And Less." for Miller Lite, and "When It Absolutely, Positively Has to Be There Overnight" for FedEx. A good commercial might last for a few years. A great campaign can last decades.

It seems to me that we are now in a third phase. After film ideas, campaign ideas, we have brand ideas. The idea is not just about creatively expressing a message about a product, it's now about finding a convincing way of communicating the present or future essence of a brand. The brand means something that the idea will sum up in a few words. For instance, here are some brand ideas devised by our network. "Think Different" for Apple. "Impossible is Nothing" for Adidas. "Shift" for Nissan. "For the Love of Dogs" for Pedigree. "Go World" for Visa. "Every Pepsi Refreshes the World" for Pepsi. "Here for Good" for Standard Chartered Bank.

It's pretty evident that such ideas are on a different scale. Their function is not just to empower an ad campaign, but to express the very essence of a brand, to give it a salient place in our minds or hearts. For ten years now, I've been encouraging our clients to adopt ideas that operate at this level. I see three reasons why this should be so.

First, by summing up the essence of what a brand stands for in a few words, we give that brand greater substance and density. It acquires emotional equity. A benefit on a higher plane. We make it part of something bigger.

The second reason is that brand ideas galvanize internally. They give a workforce energy. A strong idea resonates. Dozens of times I've shown videos of Steve Jobs, Carlos Ghosn, or Erich Stamminger praising "Think Different," "Shift," or "Impossible is Nothing." To them, these brand signatures are more than just slogans. They regard them as inspiring instructions. They use them to describe the way they want to see their company depicted, to define the mark they want it to leave, to show the furrow they intend to plough.

Finally, I place ideas at this important level for another, more technical, reason. Brand ideas are not related to any particular media, whereas campaign ideas usually are, particularly with TV. Demonstrating "Impossible is Nothing" across all media channels, whether on TV, in the papers, on the street, or especially on the Internet, is easy. This multiplies the potential for expression geometrically. A brand idea is the backbone of a communication plan. It works upstream and downstream to inspire and filter every initiative, every event, every action taken. We can say that a brand idea has the energy to drive integration.

What's the Line

People often exaggerate the impact of advertising. It's only an applied art, an approximate science. Nevertheless, when it hits the spot, it fits naturally into our everyday lives. It is the art of creating new little realities.

Tesco, the biggest food retailer in Britain, knows this well. Every initiative it takes supports its brand idea: "Every Little Helps." Tesco has been the first to think of lots of little ideas to help. Ten different types of shopping cart according to customer needs; better parking slots for families and handicapped people; more spacious restrooms, including a diaper-changing table; bar-code readers to check prices; water fountains, and cooling cabinets to keep wines and champagnes at the right temperature. More recently, Tesco launched "Freshly Clicked." You snap anything you like at home or anywhere else on your iPhone, and instantly Tesco tells you whether it's available in their stores, tells you the price, and offers to have it delivered to your home…. Despite recent ups and downs, Tesco is a model for big retailers the world over. They make a real effort. Sometimes, they seem to focus on things that aren't that important. But the desire to improve service, even at the margins, creates a dynamic. Their brand idea "Every Little Helps" puts every little improvement into perspective and makes it more meaningful. Greatness in details.

Film ideas, campaign ideas, brand ideas. Put it like that and the history makes sense. Now, we've reached a new turning point. Some people are questioning the very notion of brand idea, on the grounds that it is too restrictive to distill a brand ideal down to a brand idea. They say it gives only a partial view of reality. A facile synthesis. According to them, the time has come to lose the notion of brand ideas. They say it belongs to advertising history. Others say that in order to reflect the wealth of potential in a great brand, you need to use a collection of different slogans, offering a range of complementary themes. In France, McDonald's organizes its different initiatives into a series of distinct chapters, each of which generates a specific campaign. The advertising model is what you could call a mosaic. Every separate element is meaningful individually, and the whole draws on the strength of its component parts.

The truth is that brands need to devise their own particular models. Some will be multiple, like McDonald's. Some will remain monolithic. But I do not believe that we have come to the end of brand signatures, slogans, or campaign ideas distilled into just a few sharp words. To abandon all that would be a form of mental laziness. Those who advocate doing so are showing weakness. They're admitting to an inability to find just a few words that produce a spark in the mind. That's where our business's true craft skill lies. It's neither easy nor common. But every brand needs strong expression to rise above the crowd. "What's the line?" my boss would ask back in 1971. That question is as relevant today as it was then.

The birth of the digital age won't alter this. On the contrary. The digital world is highly fragmented. Its boundless scope for messages can dilute a brand in no time. To avoid this, we need a strong unifying brand idea. Conversely, this boundless scope can actually contribute to strengthening the brand idea. For instance, for Adidas, thousands of local initiatives gave added substance to the "Impossible is Nothing" brand idea…. Previously we were restricted in space or time by the mass media available. Now, in a digital world, we can fuel a strong central idea, strengthen it in a thousand different ways.

Food for Thought

Ideas always come from somewhere. They need feeding. They need a catalyst. They require inspiration. Strategic planning's job is to provide all this. It literally provides food for thought, as the expression goes. Planners need to offer a new angle, a specific insight. They need to weed out, interpret, fertilize their raw material to make it interesting.

But the context is changing fast. Strategic planners do much more than they used to. In the old days, their job was to ensure that their clients knew more about their potential customers than the competition: quite a task in itself. But now, they have to have expert knowledge of social networks. They need to know how to manage communities and process data and generate content…to name just a few aspects of what they do. No single human being could ever combine all that specialized knowledge. So today you have to bring together people whose expertise is complementary. When a local agency is too small to provide the resources for this, the network needs to step in to help. Each and every member of our staff, wherever they may be in the world, needs to know where they can find the help they need.

Over the last ten years, a number of observers have questioned the relevance of "old-style" networks like ours that cover some hundred or more different countries. Many people claim that all you need to do these days is operate out of a few key cities like New York, London, Shanghai, Sao Paulo, and maybe Paris. On the contrary, I believe that today's world is giving networks a new lease on life. It's strengthened them. There is talent everywhere. Social network specialists in Australia have helped our agency in LA. A graphic designer from Manila designed the layout for a luxury product handled by our Paris office. Brazilian soap opera writers based in Sao Paulo are helping content makers in our European offices. One of our Paris agencies is designing events the world over. Talent spread around the globe comes together in real time. Networks should no longer be seen as a root system, as an array of offices that collaborate from the center out, but as one giant brain that is constantly stimulated and enriched by individual input and intelligence.

One thing, though, hasn't changed. If anything, it's become truer. Planners need to cut to the chase. Out of a massive and growing quantity of information, of fact and impression, a planner's job is to cull that one thought that will stimulate those working on an account. Planners need to respect complexity but without further complicating things. A simple brief can lay the foundations for a simple campaign. A complex brief cannot.

The Holy Grail in advertising is a campaign that makes instant sense. The first time I heard "Think

Different," I just knew these simple words were right. Jonathan Ive, head of design at Apple, speaks of "inevitability." There comes a time when, if you are spot-on, what you come up with becomes unavoidable. As if it were always meant to be.

In a book I wrote twenty-five years ago, I quoted a line from the romantic composer Robert Schumann: "To compose music, all you need to do is remember a tune that no one else has ever thought of."

Japan

"Thank you very much indeed. This is a great honor for me and for Japan."

Koh Okada stood and bowed several times. The year was 1982. I was chairing the Cannes International Advertising Festival. Koh was one of twenty jury members. Hakuhodo, a big Japanese agency, had just won our Grand Prix. My vote carried no greater weight than the other nineteen jury members, but he continued to bow respectfully in my direction, as if I alone had made the decision to honor the exceptional ad the agency had submitted.

Nearly thirty years on, we are in partnership with Hakuhodo. TBWA's Tokyo office has merged with Hakuhodo's Nissan division, establishing the first major joint venture in the Japanese advertising sector. In the last ten years, I have maintained close ties with the managers of Japan's second-largest agency.

The film that won the award deserved it. It showed how National lightbulbs gave off natural seeming light.

Nowadays, the script would have called for special effects from start to finish. Back in 1982, there were almost no special effects in movies. The expression "special effects" didn't even exist. There was no trick photography in this commercial. You saw a hand slowly peeling a peach. The skin of the peach lifts slightly. Beneath the blade, you see a contrast between the damp freshness of the underside of the skin and the dry fuzz on the outside. The image is very precise. Then, gradually, beneath the skin, where the flesh ought to be, you see a shining peach-shaped light bulb. The entire sequence is shot macro. The same technical achievement is repeated with an apple. Then, more impressively still, with a single grape, the flesh of which is again a light bulb. The director's skill is riveting. The improbability of the image is fascinating. Again and again, you discover a lit light bulb nestling within the damp, cool skin of some fruit: a poetic metaphor, such as the Japanese like to use, for the parallel between the natural quality of the fruit and the natural quality of the bulb's light.

When the film was screened at Cannes, the jury fell into two camps. The Americans seemed unconvinced. The Europeans—particularly southern Europeans—gave it the Grand Prix.

As the years went by, I found myself more and more interested in Japanese advertising. I remember a giant poster suspended from Tokyo's Seibu department store. It showed a six-month-old baby swimming underwater in a pool. Near the top, you could see the surface of the water. Beneath, the baby's eyes were open as it swam. The rest of the picture was beautiful, blue water. The slogan read, "In Search of Oneself." To Japanese people, there was nothing unnatural about this image. There was nothing unusual about showing a picture of a baby swimming under water to promote a department-store relaunch. We Westerners might have seen this to be irrelevant, but to the Japanese it was appropriate.

Subtle Alchemy

Japan will always retain a degree of cultural otherness, a separateness that makes for mystery. All the same, France and Japan share a strong and ancient tradition of graphic art. Japanese and French artistic grammars have certain traits in common. Both use symbols and metaphors more than the English-speaking world.

These common traits once led me to a failure that still smarts. At the end of the 1980s, we designed a campaign for Paris department store Le Printemps that was innovative and daring and left its mark. Double-page ads brought two visuals together that weren't ever meant to be together. A left-hand page showed a woman with her arms reaching out, hands crossed. The right-hand page showed a horse's legs crossed. A left-hand page showed railroad tracks. The right-hand page showed a woman staring into the distance. A left-hand page showed hands moving symmetrically to echo the shape of plants illustrated on the right-hand side. The slogan was "Encounter Emotion." A caption read, "A department store shows you fashion, beauty, interiors, so all you have to do is listen to your five senses and feel the wonder grow."

The idea behind the campaign was to disrupt retail store convention, along the lines of the Seibu ad. We wanted to create emotion. Real emotion. Not easy in the confined space of a four-color magazine page. The desired effect was achieved by colliding emotional states: sophistication and the animal; civilization and the primitive; stillness and the living…. Advertising often just depicts emotion by showing people experiencing it. Rarely does advertising attempt to actually provoke emotion.

Our approach was unsuccessful. Drawing on Japanese advertising for a French department-store brand turned out to seem artificial. After a while, the ads stopped running. A few months later, Le Printemps left us.

Gestural Precision

In 1999, France's largest carmaker, Renault, came to the rescue of Nissan, Japan's third largest carmaker. TBWA ran the Nissan account worldwide, with the exception of Japan. The home agency was Hakuhodo. Carlos Ghosn commissioned us to bring about a convergence between Nissan's image at home and its image in the rest of the world. "One brand, one voice," he said.

People in the TBWA and Hakuhodo offices soon established an excellent relationship. The degree of mutual trust and respect was highly unusual. Western and Japanese teams found themselves working side by side. But the truth is that, for many years, they went on working parallel to each other. Despite the countless meetings, mutual influence was limited until, eventually, we came to set up a working group made up of Japanese, English, and American members, to consider the future of Infiniti. Infiniti is Nissan's upscale brand that competes with Lexus, BMW and Mercedes in America, Russia, the Middle East and now Europe.

Our Japanese partners introduced us to *Adeyaka*. Like many Japanese concepts, there is no equivalent term. It means luxury, distinction, elegance, lifestyle. It conjures up bright, powerful colors. To Japanese people, it evokes enthusiasm. In this sense, it represents the opposite of Zen values. Zen emerged as early as the late twelfth century, influencing religion, art, and every aspect of life in the archipelago. It has become a metaphor to Westerners for all things Japanese. *Adeyaka* is the counterpart. Zen is black and white, plain, minimalist, contemplative or still, and, at the end of the day, stereotyped. *Adeyaka*, on the other hand, is vibrant, colorful, fluent, warm, imaginative, dynamic, and fascinating. When I compared the difference between Zen and *Adeyaka* styles to our difference between classical and baroque, my Japanese friends called me out on this. The comparison, they said, was too coarse. Apart from anything else, *Adeyaka* belongs to now, not the past.

135

The designers behind Infiniti found inspiration in the traditions of *Adeyaka*. We often discussed this with them. This led to the writing of a manifesto where we spoke of the force of nature, of vibrant colors and refined craftsmanship. Our first commercial took as its starting point the most famous gesture in Japan, the gesture a calligrapher performs when, after several minutes' concentration, in a fraction of a second, he produces a line that curves across the page. The motion is swift, like a judo move. Talent, temperament, and also considerable experience are required to achieve the right degree of precision. Our film concluded with the words "From a single line comes Infiniti."

I believe we were able to grasp the spirit of *Adeyaka*. We avoided the severity of Zen imagery. At the same time, we were offering something different from the cold, mechanical world of German car manufacturers. I was told that, in Japan, people smile when they say the word *Adeyaka*.

Tradition of Respect

I like Japan. But despite visiting Tokyo dozens of times, I find I still do not understand Japanese people well. Japanese culture is remote to ours. Reading the minds of men and women from a culture so different from your own is always hard. One thing, though, I do know. Japanese people's thirst for knowledge is boundless. An old observation has it that "Japanese people are born Shinto, think Confucianism, and die Buddhist." The Japanese think of themselves as a people that likes to absorb things. They like to appropriate anything foreign that seems interesting. The minute I arrive in Japan, I am bombarded with questions. People want to know what's going on in the global advertising scene. The Japanese market is pretty much in a world of its own.

I know what most of the Japanese people think of French people. They think we're ill mannered and overtalkative. They think we don't understand that in a conversation, silence is fine. And the truth is that I have never succeeded in avoiding the pitfall that comes from being asked so many questions. I always end up talking more than the people I'm with. Even though I can't help remembering, as a meeting draws to a close, that they have more respect for those people who talk less.

I have nevertheless made friends with some of my Japanese colleagues, particularly Miyachi-san. After running several agency departments, he has just gone into retirement. Back in 1999, he was running the Nissan account. From day one, he showed a remarkable degree of openness toward us. Together, we overcame many obstacles. And over the course of our many fine, long Japanese suppers we have had many conversations. He taught me the key value in Japan, the value that rules and includes all others in Japanese people's minds, which is respect.

People in Japan are known for their reserve, their discretion. Their manners are formal. Their way of never saying no can cause misunderstandings. They do not always agree with what Westerners suggest, so by never saying no, they can appear two-faced. But to their way of thinking, differentiating between superficial attitudes (*Tatemae*) and deeper truths (*Honne*) reflects a necessary detachment that shows courtesy. As I was taught by Ayami Nakao, a top executive at Hakuhodo who is also a close friend, wanting to get to the essence of the person you're talking to too fast is disrespectful. Japanese people's favorite tree is called *sakura*. It is the slowest to blossom, but when it does blossom, the blooms are incomparable.

Japanese people show greatest respect toward their closest colleagues. Observers are often wrong in believing that Japanese organizations are hierarchical. In fact, American-style top-down management does not really exist in Japan. Relationships are based on mutual respect. What counts are the contributions people make to their immediate circle. If you ask a Japanese person where he works, he won't say Sony or Nissan. He'll say in the research department at Sony or in the design division at Nissan. Japanese people feel bound to their departments more than to their corporations. They feel a commitment toward those closest to them. They are known for their group mentality. But the truth is that they are possessed of team spirit. They have the most respect for the person nearest to them.

When it comes to nature, respect changes to veneration. I wrote the following sentences several months before the disaster at Fukushima. On rereading, I have not felt they needed changing. I do not believe that, at heart, this gigantic disaster has altered Japanese people's feeling for nature. It will prove to be just another trauma in the long history of cataclysms that has made Japan what it is. Those cataclysms have brought Japanese people, at the very deepest level, into peculiar osmosis with forces beyond their understanding. They show limitless deference for nature. They worship nature. It is their first source of inspiration. Nature guides Japan and terrifies it. Japanese people believe that spirits inhabit every grain, every drop of rain, every pebble and stone. As Miyachi-san once told me, "In Japan, human art must always follow the art of nature."

One day, he summed up this thinking in the following way: "In my country, we respect nature, we respect people, we respect respect."

Though we were always on the brink of friendship, until my sixtieth birthday, I considered my relationship with Miyachi-san and his Japanese colleagues essentially professional. Then when I turned sixty, they sent me a video and a few gifts. The video told me that *kanreki*, second childhood, begins in one's sixty-first year. The Japanese characters for *kanreki* combine two meanings, return and calendar. A sixtieth birthday is not just any birthday. It represents the end of one sixty-year cycle and the start of the next. The cycle ends when each of the twelve signs of the zodiac has passed through each of the five elements: water, fire, earth, wood, and metal. In Japan, *kanreki* is rebirth.

Tradition has it that the person celebrating his sixtieth birthday must don a red cloak and a broad red hat. My Japanese friends sent me these garments. Red is the color babies wear in Japan. By sending me these gifts, they were celebrating my rebirth.

Knockout

"BDDP is dead."

We were sitting around in a circle in high-backed, reproduction sixteenth-century armchairs when Michel Pébereau, the chief executive of BNP, the biggest bank in France, told us the game was over. The agency Jean-Claude Boulet, Marie-Catherine Dupuy, Jean-Pierre Petit, and I had set up ten years earlier was about to fall to outsiders. Despite its considerable success in the market.

The cold brutality of his words filled the room. He started out by saying, "I have four things to say to you." He stated that BDDP was dead. He went on to tell us that we were being sold to Havas. He reminded us—this was the third point—that we had offered our personal guarantees for the company's debts. In other words, we were to have no say in what was happening. Or else most of our future income would be given over to repaying debt for as long as this might take, which could be a very long time. Finally, he told us he had no time to lose: "I need your formal agreement by Monday morning." This was Friday evening.

141

We refused. We turned his buyer down. To this day, I wonder how we were able to manage the stress of the months and years that followed.

I no longer bear any grudge against Michel Pébereau. I sometimes meet him at Paris's Institute of Political Science, where we both teach. Time heals everything. But I do resent the system. I resent the divine right our era has granted big banks. I note the disdain their managers often display toward clients. I observe the immunity they are skilled at obtaining for themselves. Bankers have forgotten they are intermediaries. And nothing more. Their job is to act as intermediaries between a resource—money—and those who need it, their clients, who are not beholden to them.

This was the way we portrayed the banking profession in the film we made for the BNP privatization. Though we were engaged in these unpleasant negotiations with BNP, somehow we still had the mental resources to win the pitch for their privatization campaign—a crucial juncture in their history. In the nineties, many French companies were still state owned. A process of privatization handed them back to the general public by stock-market listing. BNP was one of these companies. The commercial we made was inspired by the improbable sculptures of Tinguely, who became famous with making structures of wheels within wheels, turning inside each other like giant clockwork. Our commercial showed a young boy pedaling a bicycle, creating the energy to give life to buildings and factories. It was a metaphor for a bank's contribution to the economy. Michel Pébereau told me he appreciated the analogy.

We had accumulated too much debt. Nine hundred million francs (two hundred million dollars at the then exchange rate). We had set out to conquer the world. We had tried to build a global network, based on our success in Paris and our knowledge of the way networks functioned from our years at Young & Rubicam. We had done too much too fast. The world champion of self-fulfilling prophecy, Martin Sorrell, CEO at WPP, was telling people consolidation was about to hit the advertising business big time. He claimed this was being imposed upon him. In reality, he was the driving force behind it.

This constant talk of consolidation drove us into thinking, "We've only got a few years in which to act." As I already explained, New York's third-biggest agency, Wells Rich Greene, and its prestigious client list were up for sale. We didn't hesitate.

Slow Death

Commentators said we were overly ambitious. I don't believe that. We weren't presumptuous. We were bold. We almost got away with it. But a set of unlucky coincidences struck us all at the same time. Several of our biggest American clients hit us with massive and simultaneous budget cuts. Our second-biggest client filed for Chapter 11. We also had fraud problems within the New York ranks. All these things happened within a few weeks of one another during the summer of 1993. O.J. Simpson, the football star turned actor, was our Hertz campaign spokesperson.

Not long after, he was indicted for the murder of his wife. Stunned TV audiences from around the world watched helicopter footage of his purported getaway drive. Overnight, Hertz's CEO canceled every single forthcoming campaign.

In 1989, we had been planning a stock exchange flotation in order to fund our international development. The economic climate meant postponing those plans. Then came the Wells opportunity. The timing was bad but we were afraid no such opportunity would ever come up again. We took a gamble. We funded the acquisition entirely through long-term debt. The leverage, as it turned out, was too heavy for us.

Maybe we were too bold. But we were encouraged by our many advisors to be so. Financial experts of all sorts—bankers, investment fund managers, middlemen in all shapes and sizes—were lining up outside my partner Jean-Claude Boulet's office. Just a few months earlier, we had talked about buying J. Walter Thompson, one of the biggest networks in the world. Jean-Claude had gone so far as head-hunting the man he wanted to put in charge: a former JWT executive named Burt Manning. We had found the money. Or nearly: as it turned out, we were only a hundred million dollars or so short. In the end, Martin Sorrell bought JWT, which was the first of his many acquisitions. A few weeks later, Jean-Claude and I were chatting with a manager from First Boston in New York. Martin Sorrell had just told him that JWT's Tokyo building was on the balance sheet at the incredibly low value of ten million dollars. He sold it instantly for two hundred five million dollars, considerably reducing the effective cost of his acquisition. This was just one of a long series of lucky breaks in Martin Sorrell's life. It was also an illustration of the J. Walter Thompson previous management's amateurism. It gave us something to regret. It showed us we could have made it.... Oh and also: Martin Sorrell hired Burt Manning to run JWT.

I often say "we nearly made it" to describe our feelings at the time. We were living on a knife edge. Financially speaking. Commercially speaking. Very soon, we became aware of the fact that Mary Wells's successors in managing her company weren't up to the mark. But we couldn't face the upheaval of removing them. We thought that would scare off possible investors. We had to first of all resolve our problem of undercapitalization. Since we didn't succeed, time passed, and the weakness of the New York management led to the loss of a number of clients. And talent. We were caught in a vicious circle that became untenable.

The financial markets put a stop to our adventure. Investors entered into negotiations with the banks and took over the company. They placed it in the hands of a man who owned a hedge fund. This was in 1994. We were his first big job, his passport into the inner circle. Thanks to us, he was able to make an entrance into the hallowed world of Private Equity. No doubt that is why he was so nervous and intemperate at the time. Let's just say we were unlucky enough to have him cut his teeth on us. The rest of this sorry tale can be told in just a few words. As expected, our new shareholder was not with us for long. He put us up for sale barely

145

two years after the acquisition. This was a terrible upheaval: too soon after our previous shock; a second death, really.

The moneymen brought an injection of misery. We had been naïve. We discovered their deviousness, the three-handed poker they played. It made me sick that our company was up for sale again. I couldn't prevent myself from voicing vehement protest. One of our new "friends" said, "What are you complaining about? Of course I go back on my word after I've given it. Otherwise I would have none left." That just about says it all.

What strikes me still, fifteen years later, is not that we lost the company we founded. It's the verbal abuse we had to put up with in the process. Losing the company was always a possibility. But the humiliation, meeting after meeting, the insults leveled at us in front of our lawyers at two in the morning, remain very vivid in my mind. I didn't expect the smooth world of finance to contain such brutally rough language.

Anyway. We lose the company. Seven years pass. I am put in charge of TBWA. I still wonder how I survived those seven years. The answer is, I like what I do. I won't say I am passionate about it. That would be an exaggeration. Researchers, professors, inventors are passionate. Steve Jobs was passionate. Apple's board threw him out. When they were forced to hire him back, he gave the *Wall Street Journal* an interview in which he discussed passion: "People say you have to have a lot of passion for what you're doing and it's totally true. And the reason is because it's so hard that if you don't, any rational person would give up. It's really hard. And you have to do it over a sustained period of time. So if you don't love it, if you're not having fun doing it, you're going to give up. And that's what happens to most people, actually."

The truth is, we never gave up.

Two Economies

Around the same time we were having our adventures in the world of high finance, in 1996, a very well-known French philosopher named Jean Baudrillard wrote a prophetic piece. He offered a vision of the world of money as an independent entity in orbit, spinning around the world at dizzying speeds. The speed was in proportion to the exponential increase in financial transactions that occurs every second. Down beneath, at the earth's surface, lay the real economy. The two economies, financial and real, were disconnected. And if any short circuit had happened to bring them back into contact, there had to be a big bang, an unavoidable crash.

The metaphor makes more sense in Baudrillard's own words: "Debt moves in its own orbit. Its trajectory is totally autonomous. It is capital freed of any actual economic contingency. It moves in a parallel universe, preserved by constant acceleration, from crashing back down into the dull world of production, value and usage.... The probability of this universe rejoining ours is very low." And also: "The real satellites circling our planet are world debt, free-floating capital, nuclear ammunition carving their ever-circling ring around the earth." And finally: "All these parallel universes, locked into their autonomous and exponential systems, are time bombs. That's an obvious thing to say about nuclear devices, but it's true about debt and free-floating capital too. Anytime those worlds re-enter our atmosphere, anytime their orbit encounters ours, the fragile equilibrium of our exchanges and our economies will shatter."

It happened. Those orbits did come into collision. The last crash was the most violent. It was also the third or fourth crash since Baudrillard wrote that piece. Successive recessions have shown once and for all that capitalism needs crises. It feeds off crises to then rebound. But the crises are getting more and more frequent. Because the financial bubble has become so huge.

One of the results is that banks are undercapitalized. The idea that vital increases in capital should be made compulsory has bank chairmen yelling. Shamelessly and without qualms, they reply that if banks are forced to set aside a greater proportion of their revenues to recapitalize, then there'll be less money available to support the economy, which will adversely affect companies by starving them of the credit they need.

The line of argument they use is irrefutable. Except that, for twenty years now, banks have been failing to increase their equity. For twenty years, they've been handing out too great a part of their profits, allowing the assets to shareholder equity ratio to slip perilously. The chief executive of Lazards Bank in Paris, Mathieu Pigasse, states the obvious: "Bankers are supposed to evaluate other people's credit risk. Nowadays, they don't even know how to assess their own."

Necessity of the Long Term

Criticizing the financial world's "short termism" has become commonplace. Especially where market speculation is concerned. Algorithmic trading now means that operations can be conducted to a hundred thousandth of a second. My own belief is that certain corporate leaders are also at fault. They have taken to ignoring the need for long-term vision and accepted the dictates of their financial counterparts. Some board members regard corporations as a mere accumulation of assets to be assembled or disassembled at will, according to stock-market fashions.

Restoring long-term values is vital. Boards need to stop paying mere lip service to them. They need to stop asset stripping, closing plants, dismantling them for short-term profit. So many investment funds are experts at that and that alone. So many voluntary or forced company CEO resignations result. This has to come to an end if we are to compete against emerging nation companies supported by governments obsessed with the long term. In Asia, business looks ahead decades.

One thing is indispensable. In the Western world, the pace of the economy needs to lengthen its stride once more, and the pace of finance, which has become too frenetic, needs to slow down. The economy and finance need to get back into sync. That won't happen until there is a real shift inside corporations. Any barrier that stands in the way of that shift should be removed. Starting with the excessive influence short-term financial thinking has on strategic decision-making.

Our agency represents a bank that considers itself different. This is Standard Chartered Bank, a London-based corporation with a strong presence in Asia. In the middle of the worst recession in more than half a century, it has just published its seventh year of consecutive profits. Prudent investment policies allowed it to avoid the bubble that has damaged so many of its competitors. A unique culture of "doing the right thing" has also proved beneficial. It was, for instance, the first international bank to return to Afghanistan when other banks resolutely stayed far away. We have just produced a striking campaign for Standard Chartered. The theme is "Here for Good," to emphasize that the bank is in it for the long term. But many parallel meanings emerged. Indeed, the voice-over commentary to the films we made reads like a manifesto. Here it is:

Can a bank really stand for something?
Can it balance its ambition with its conscience?
To do what it must. Not what it can.
As not everything in life that counts can be counted.
Can it not only look at the profit it makes

but how it makes that profit?
And stand beside people, not above them.
Where every solution depends on each person.
Simply by doing good, can a bank in fact be great?
In the many places we call home,
  our purpose remains the same.
To be here for people.
Here for progress.
Here for the long run.
Here for good.

We made three films for this campaign, each providing a different illustration for this commentary. One of them, my favorite, was directed by a young Ethiopian artist, Ezra Wube. The way he made this commercial was unique. He shot just a few painted images on canvas. A brushstroke here, a rag wiping a corner of canvas gradually transformed the pictures, providing a snapshot of each successive stage. Three months' work generated more than one thousand shots. One thousand paintings, in fact. It's a superb piece of filmmaking.

Ezra Wube gave the money he made to an Ethiopian school. The soundtrack, composed by an African group, was released. The film was first broadcast in China. Releasing an African film on Chinese screens for a UK-headquartered bank is an elegant tale of globalization.

When Peter Sands, group CEO of Standard Chartered Bank, read the text of the voice-over commentary, he said, "I want our seventy thousand people to internalize this, so they can recite it by heart." That was his way of encouraging every member of staff to do what he or she can to ensure the bank practices what it preaches.

Never would I have imagined that one day I would find it natural for a bank to pose the question: "Can a bank be great?"

Luxury

"Forget luxury goods, especially perfume."

This was the mid-eighties. LVMH and PPR, the world's two leading luxury corporations, both of them French, were nothing like what they are now. Most luxury advertising was for perfumes. We had just started our agency. During one management committee meeting, we established a list of clients we wanted to target. We excluded perfume makers.

We'd had some unhappy experiences. The perfume industry is creative, complex, and subtle, and many perfume makers don't see what advertising talent has to offer. Agencies work with ideas. Perfume makers create territories. I mean a world of impressions, memories, tremulous mystery. The scent itself, or *jus* as people in the business call it, is just a means of stimulating and giving understanding to what the bottle and name are supposed to inspire. In this context, agency ideas seem inappropriate. They seem like a betrayal of perfume makers' notions of territory. As if they're introducing superfluous elements into their world.

We didn't understand each other.

To the people in the perfume business, advertising was just an unavoidable stage near the end of the process. For them, it was creative, but only in a minor way. Even the most prestigious perfume makers seemed satisfied with overly conformist advertising. Fashion magazines had ended up looking like fragrance catalogues, stuffed with page after page of forgettable advertisements for different perfumes. I found it sad that so much upstream talent and labor should result in such clichés. And that is why, in our early days, we avoided working for the luxury industry.

Then one day in 1986, we were visited by two ladies who had set up an agency improbably called Mafia, then number one in the luxury sector in France. Everyone longed to acquire their company. They chose us. We couldn't refuse. Thanks to them, we attended several Yves Saint Laurent shows, when he was at the height of his art. Little by little, we came to understand a world that had been alien to us. And so our agency became familiar first with the world of fragrance, then fashion and luxury.

Twenty-five years later, it is no exaggeration to say that the luxury sector's approach to marketing is permeating business all around the world. There has been a shift to a more complex, more fluid and diverse approach to marketing that stands in opposition to the more monolithic and simplistic classical tradition. There is probably more to be learned today from Hermès than from General Motors, from Dior than from Unilever. Luxury marketing modes may one day become the benchmark. It has long been instinctive for Europeans to believe that a brand must be more than just a name for a product or range of products. They know that brands should not be restricted to specific products, but should have a life of their own. Brands need constant renewal, constant nourishment. America invented the discipline of marketing. Europe has taken the science of brands to a new level.

Our apprenticeship in the world of luxury had its high points. One of these dates back to the earliest days of our collaboration with Mafia. With British director Ridley Scott, we shot a memorable film for Saint Laurent. An enraged Linda Evangelista has run out of Opium. She plunges into the slums of a Far Eastern city in search of a dose of the heady perfume. She discovers a bottle in the back of a den, hands over a stack of bills, and the film ends on a signature, "Opium, for addicts."

I have to say this rattled me. It seemed to break every rule in the book of luxury product advertising. Defining territories is about suggestion, not overt statement. It's about impression, not narrative. Obviousness is definitely out. Yves Saint Laurent had had the audacity to call his scent Opium. So what was the point in showing the adventures of a woman in the Golden Triangle? Too much realism kills magic. But the film was a hit. This undermined my certainties. I learned that even in perfumes there is no such thing as an unbreakable rule. Opium was so original it could afford to be obvious.

The years go by. Twenty-five years later, we have just finished making a film that has created a certain impact. I'm referring to the new film for Dior's "J'Adore" scent. Backstage at a fashion show, you see Charlize Theron getting ready. She puts on her makeup. She slips into her clothes. She is with Grace Kelly, Marlene Dietrich, and Marilyn Monroe. It is a story that builds a bridge between haute couture and the perfume business as never before. It was shot in the Hall of Mirrors at the Sun King's Palace of Versailles, outside Paris. It clearly signals the House of Dior's couture heritage, plunging deep into the brand's timeless and eternal origins. I believe this may be the first time the glamorous environment of a fashion show has been used as the setting for perfume advertisement. This pays beautiful tribute to the brand's iconic haute-couture dimension.

Luxury vs. Premium

I've talked about Tag Heuer, the Swiss watch company. We produced three spectacular campaigns for Tag Heuer over ten years, designed around three different slogans: "Don't Crack Under Pressure," "Success is a Mind Game," and "What Are You Made Of?" Some of our visuals ended up on the cover of trade magazines: a sprinter leaping over a hurdle made of razor blades; relay runners passing sticks of live dynamite; sailors tacking across the edge of Niagara Falls...arresting images. Watch sales shot up. And average sale prices doubled, then tripled. Some people said we propelled Tag Heuer into the luxury watch category. I don't believe this is so. We didn't bring about that leap of the imagination that spells luxury. I don't think a brand like Tag Heuer can do that. It doesn't have the heritage. All we did was help build a brand that could justify charging a much higher price for its products.

Tag Heuer taught me something Vincent Bastien and Jean-Noël Kapferer recently described in their book, *Luxury Strategy*. One of the chapters is entitled "The End of a Confusion: Premium is Not Luxury." Premium brands extend ordinary marketing techniques upmarket. Luxury brands think differently. Often, they behave in quite the opposite way to premium brands. Luxury brands are less concerned by sales volume. The obsession is not to sell more. The obsession lies elsewhere.

Take Infiniti. I have already discussed how this upmarket Nissan brand competes with Toyota's Lexus. We spent a lot of time debating the distinction between premium brands and luxury brands with Nissan management. Infiniti represents the essence of premium branding. Its models are exceptionally engineered for reliability and exceptionally daring in their design. The high price is justified, although Infiniti is not yet a luxury brand...It comes with no heritage to speak of. It lacks the kind of depth that only comes with time. No Lexus or Infiniti customer would ever visit the factory where their vehicle is made. By comparison, two-thirds of all Rolls Royce customers pick up their new car in person at the factory. In our work for Infiniti, we're not giving Infiniti the trappings of luxury. We just want to show what the cars are worth. To demonstrate that Infiniti is worth the high asking price.

We're selling premium products here. Very premium, in fact. But as Pierre Bergé, Yves Saint Laurent's partner, used to say, luxury does not deal with products but with objects. A Rolls Royce is an object. So is a Ferrari.

The Paradox of Luxury

It could possibly appear somewhat simplistic attaching so much importance to the past when defining luxury. As if all you need to say was "established such-and-such a year" to qualify. Shang Xia, the Chinese luxury brand set up by Hermès, has been around for just a couple of years. But its identity is built on a very high degree of craft excellence. It is a reflection of a centuries-old tradition. That's the important part. It's not the history; it's the heritage a luxury brand needs. Heritage is credible if it embodies traditions handed down. It is associated with long-preserved craft practices that are both sophisticated and exclusive. True luxury brands have long memories.

They also need to think ahead. To be part of the avant-garde. They need to anticipate tomorrow's trends. The boldest of them behave with a habit of unpredictability. They do not progress in a linear fashion but search in all directions. John Galliano, former artistic director at Dior, used to travel the world in between shows clutching a tiny suitcase

158

crammed with photographs, notes, and sketches. A fleeting instant seized in an unlikely place at the far end of the planet provided extravagant inspiration for the next collection. John Galliano never betrayed the spirit of Christian Dior because Dior thought of each collection as a spectacular gesture, a seasonal disruption. He did not believe in happy mediums. People said that Christian Dior was the embodiment of "bold elegance," which at the time, in 1947, seemed like a contradiction in terms.

One thing all couture houses, and by extension all luxury brands, have in common is the ability to juxtapose contradictions. They steer from one paradox to the next. They thrive on paradox. They need to feed on the past without ever falling into a caricature of themselves. They need to attract attention while maintaining distance. They need to address a narrow and elitist customer base, but they need to be famous and acknowledged and celebrated the world over. They can afford to raise their prices without losing sales because their customers hate the idea that the value of their objects is slipping. They offer limited editions because they need to create rarity, whereas most manufacturers do all they can to avoid out-of-stock situations. Luxury brand sales have exploded, reaching mass-market levels, without losing the glamour of distinction. Subtle touch by subtle touch, they remain exclusive.

And yet, by descending to street level in such an ostentatious manner, they risk becoming too familiar. The ultimate paradox is this: every sale imperceptibly diminishes brand appeal.

Establishing a luxury brand involves treading a narrow path between the pitfalls and contradictions of the genre, constantly developing new rule-breaking ideas. Creative talent is there to preserve an overall coherence, a sense of continuity. The yardstick is intuitive. When their creative intuition crystallizes what connoisseurs expect, creative talent becomes idolized. Creative eccentricity becomes revered as reference. At the same time, creative talent must come with innate competence. Lagerfeld and Gaultier were a natural fit at Chanel and Hermès respectively. At that level, talent is not self-conscious. The mind wanders intuitively wherever it must, invariably finding what is just.

Creative talent often needs an alter ego, a shadow at its side. When the head of the company is of the same sensibility as the creative designer, the sky's the limit. At Louis Vuitton, for instance, Yves Carcelle's cheerful discipline has proved a great match for Marc Jacobs's cultural eclecticism.

Yves Carcelle joined Vuitton in 1990. He was one of the first people to recognize the emergence of a wealthy segment of the population in developing countries and a general increase in purchasing power of the middle classes in the developed world. Both of which would generate growth markets for the luxury sector. Early on, too, he realized the threat that increased sales could strip the glamour from a product. He has taken Louis Vuitton a very long way. But he has had the intelligence to move forward one step at a time. One initiative at a time. One store at a time. One show at a time.

Yves Carcelle spends more than half his time visiting Louis Vuitton's global 448-store network. He makes sure that the spirit of Vuitton is constantly being renewed throughout. He hates the idea of a single formula being applied globally. Luxury cannot afford to be repetitious. His latest London store, on New Bond Street, bears scant resemblance to the Champs-Elysées flagship in Paris. The VIP area contains a picture by Jean-Michel Basquiat, a mirror by Jeff Koons, photographs by Richard Prince, a stained-glass window by Gilbert & George, and many other artworks. Strolling through the store, you can sense the spirit of the forthcoming Louis Vuitton Foundation, due to open as a museum in 2012 and designed by Frank Gehry.

Louis Vuitton's chief executive was the first person in the luxury business to open a store in Ulan Bator. He is always first in providing a reference point for others. Few of us know that Mongolia's population of three million is living on a goldmine or, to be more precise, on gigantic radium and other precious metal reserves. Yves Carcelle believes that this desert land is heading for a Gulf-style future.... He was also the first person to bet on the cities of inland China, venturing further than just the big coastal cities. In 2010, Louis Vuitton opened boutiques in some thirty-five inland Chinese cities.... I remember the original Paris store in a smart, quiet street called Avenue Marceau. I must have entered it for the first time some thirty or forty years ago, never imagining what the future had in store.

It's been an impressive story. Louis Vuitton is the flagship brand of LVMH group, whose stock market worth is today ten times that of major French car manufacturer Peugeot Citroën. This is a fact that my daughter, who's twenty, doesn't find at all surprising. But to my generation, brought on up the heavy industrial drive of the postwar years, that differential seems scarcely believable. Louis Vuitton was a pioneer. French companies today represent some 50 percent of the world luxury market. A fine instance of what French people like to call "l'exception culturelle," their cultural difference.

Luxury as a Business Model

Mass-market brands have a lot to learn from the luxury trade. Traditional marketing was developed to make the most of mass media. It was all about "positioning." In other words, all about reducing a product to its most salient characteristic. To what makes it stand out. A thirty-second commercial could only get one big idea across. Selecting that idea meant abandoning all other ideas. Luxury brands don't need to make that decision. They are inclusive of everything.

Consumer goods' brand managers put all their effort into what they call "putting the customer back at the center of things." They seek inspiration from the consumer, from outside the company. But, as is well known, customers cannot lead companies in what they should be doing. That's why the only kind of marketing that is really effective is the one that works from the inside out. The reality is that successful new product ideas can only come out of the intuition and talent of the person in charge of the brand. This is precisely the way things work in the luxury sector. Brands don't follow clients; they're one step ahead of them. They know that inspiration has to come from themselves, from within the company, not outside it.

Another important factor is that luxury brands are skilled at building perceptions over and above the actual products they sell. Chanel and Dior mean much more than dresses and scent. In the luxury business, brand comes before product. It exists in isolation, for its own sake. Yet at the same time, in no other sector do products play such an important part in fashioning the spirit of a brand. Much more than anywhere else, the reciprocal energy between product and brand is flagrant.

In short, the luxury goods business works in a way that is qualitatively different from, not to say opposed to, the way packaged goods markets work. Procter & Gamble or Unilever started out as household goods businesses. They diversified into skincare products. Now they are competing in the market for luxury products by purchasing top perfume brands. The people who run Procter and Unilever are doing their best to understand markets that are about increasing profit margins as far as possible, even if that means lower sales volumes. They realize that luxury means building brands differently. They know that in the luxury sector, brands lie at the heart of a delicate web of references. Complexity is a virtue.

New ideas come from sharing an original view on the world. Or a different way of moving through it. The luxury business is all about this. Its approach is rooted in the time-honored tradition, the craft skills of the ancient continent of Europe. This leads to a more holistic, less monolithic approach.

Our way of doing things is specific to Europe. It has been honed over time. Group dynamics in business meetings in Paris are not growing more similar, as you might expect, to the way such meetings are conducted in New York, but less. The references are not the same. The association of ideas travels along different lines. So much depends on where you start out from, on asking a specific question, on individual and group reflexes that are the products of years of experience, on a shared intuition that prompts tacit understanding. However tenuous this may seem, I firmly believe that our way of entering into a subject, our way of approaching new territory, is one of the most powerful weapons we have across the Atlantic Ocean in Europe. I see it in action every day.

Media Arts

"From 360 to 365."

This expression offers a good description of the upheaval experienced in our business recently. For a couple of decades now, people in advertising have been referring to "360," meaning 360-degree integration, an expression first used by Ogilvy & Mather. Integration refers to our ability to orchestrate every different type of communication: advertising, public relations, event marketing, customer relationship management, digital, etc. To be heard, a brand must speak with only one voice. The people at Ogilvy were pioneers in this respect. To them the critical issue was that no brand expression should ever step out of line. Hence the 360 idea.

Navigating Through Time

The years have gone by. We have entered a new digital era. Internet offers new scope. These days, different brand expressions rub shoulders with each other, enrich and complement one another. Promotional events become advertising that generates press commentary that gets picked up on social networks.... These different interactions are not haphazard and need to be managed.

The pace of work has accelerated beyond recognition. Ten years ago, annual advertising plans were sacred. Now they rarely go as planned. They are constantly being revised. Reality impinges every day to alter the course of things. Our media environment, especially the World Wide Web, is forcing us to react at a moment's notice. So the issue is no longer merely ensuring that the brand is consistent in all its various manifestations, but nourishing a year-round constant conversation with our audiences. Not so much orchestrating communication through space—that is, 360 degrees—as navigating through time, 365 days of the year.

One of our agencies was way ahead of the game in this. Up to one hundred and twenty staff worked full time on the Adidas account in Amsterdam, generating every major Adidas campaign around the world. No agency was as news-responsive, as news-sensitive as these people. The teams would gather in a room with a wall calendar over fifteen feet long that listed every important sporting event in the world over a six-month period. Driven by the brand's guiding idea that "Impossible is Nothing," each team member would think of how to get Adidas involved in those upcoming events. What were they going to do about the Rugby World Cup Final? What would they be saying if the world 100-meter sprint champion ran in Adidas shoes? They also scanned the previous days' events, generating a range of fresh responses to what had been happening. It was like the morning conference in a newspaper's newsroom. Indeed, Larry Light, former McDonald's head of marketing, says everything a brand does is a story waiting to be told. You need to communicate, he says, day in, day out. "Brand journalism" is a term he uses.

Brands generate editorial content. Everything the brand does can fuel its content. If consumers are interested, a dialogue begins. Often, this takes the form of an exchange between reality and virtual reality. A constant to-ing and fro-ing. As an example, a street event is created. It goes on the Internet. And from there, it is turned back into a TV commercial. Saatchi's T-Mobile campaign was a classic of the genre. Hundreds of people had been contacted by mobile phone and asked to join a dozen professional dancers under the high vaults of Liverpool Street Station, in London. They all danced together for ten minutes according to a tight choreography. Amazed onlookers joined in. Immediately, the video was uploaded onto the Net. The same video, cut down to forty-five seconds, became a TV ad for T-Mobile.... Interactions of this sort take place in every direction. Any activity can feed into any other. Interactions develop and spread organically, never twice in the same way.

More than merely orchestrating activity in space, navigating in time calls for imagination and creativity. It requires a new kind of intellectual agility. It brings a sense of jubilation; there is real pleasure in seeing wheels spin within wheels, in telling stories whose twists and turns are never the same.

Complement to Disruption

Making the most of these exciting new possibilities requires a novel approach to managing resources. We call it Media Arts. I am not referring to the "Media Arts Lab" now, which is where we run the Apple account in LA. I mean something different: an innovative way of managing every aspect of what we do in our network, every day. The name comes in two parts. "Media" because analyzing all forms of media has become central once again. And "Arts" because what matters is the care and invention that go into shaping every point of contact between a brand and its audiences. "Gracefully, artfully" is how we like to put it.

Any activity, any expression that carries a brand's name, must reflect what the brand believes in. Whether it's Apple's store architecture. Or, more prosaically, Pedigree's packaging. It took us a long time to convince our client to change it. We kept at them because we knew packaging mattered, whereas in the old days we might have decided it was none of our business. So the expression "Media Arts" is a reminder to everyone in our offices that communication for any brand is only as effective as the weakest link in the chain. Whether that link is a TV film, an event, a website, packaging or whatever, Media Arts is a perfectly simple description of what we are trying to achieve. Having the right words to precisely describe what it is you are attempting to do gives you more confidence to let your imagination run free in doing it.

Media Arts encourages new ways of thinking. Not always starting with a thirty-second commercial. Maybe an interactive idea might be more effective. Or a public relations operation. The ways ideas develop and unfold are different these days. With social networks on the one hand, apps on the other, there are thousands of new ways of starting a conversation. So thinking about which media to use and when has taken center stage again. It's a starting point. We need to think very carefully about where new and old media fit into our lives. We need a very precise understanding of how today's world consumes media, if we want our brand ideas to be able to travel freely and efficiently through them.

When the time comes to define a new communications plan, a new road map for a brand, we like to begin with a Media Arts Day, modeled on our Disruption Days. We use a set of exercises to think of all the different ways a brand might come in contact with its public. The two methods are complementary. Disruption is upstream: it tells us what a brand stands for, what it believes. Media Arts is downstream: it defines the way a brand is going to behave. The terms used are "Brand Belief" and "Brand Behavior." One goes inextricably with the other.

Non-Paid Media

When we hold Media Arts Days, one of the things we concentrate on is non-paid media. For decades, agencies focused on bought media, on advertisers' considerable investment in TV, radio, newspapers and magazines, posters, and the Internet. But there are many other media at our disposal. Sometimes, we can exploit media a brand may actually own. Railroad operators, for instance, own billboard networks. Apple owns Apple Stores, which are a unique form of medium. In addition, a brand can also generate its own media. It can produce an iPhone app, set up a radio station as we did for Snickers, or create retail space, like the Pedigree Adoption Drive store on New York's Fifth Avenue. There are also truly free media, generated by the public or the traditional media around unusual events. When three hundred international TV channels broadcast reports on the Adidas-organized football game on a Tokyo rooftop, the—free—value to the brand was estimated in tens of millions of dollars.

I don't know who it was in America who came up with the four distinct terms we now use to distinguish these different types of media: paid, owned, created, and earned. But these definitions have now been adopted by the industry. There has been a paradigm shift. Today, media planners regard non-paid media as being on an equal footing with paid media. Paid media (TV, print, radio, etc.) may still be indispensable, but they are also expensive. So they are coming to be seen

170

as complementary to other cheaper forms of media. Today we think about how a TV commercial is going to dramatically increase traffic on a brand's website. How a geolocalized billboard with a QR code is going to multiply store traffic. How a commercial in a multiplex cinema is going to generate social network buzz. So classic media are no longer considered in the same way. They're seen as catalysts now. They are not always the lead factor in a media plan. Sometimes they are just there to reinforce it.

The rumor mill, gossip, buzz are no longer just a product of media strategy. They're an upstream component. People used to talk of "press impact," which, as the name implies, happened after the event. Now, as in the T-Mobile example, an event can actually be a starting point. Reporters, opinion makers, trendsetters, consumers pick it up and take it on from there. Gradually, the importance of word of mouth is being restored to its position prior to mass media's arrival. It's back in the number-one spot.

You need to know where to start. I'm a great believer in events as a starting point. Street events, like T-Mobile Dance. Stadium events, like Gatorade Replay. Tokyo rooftop events, like Adidas Sky Soccer. Events launch an idea. They create the buzz that gives a brand energy way before it hits classic media. Events send a brand into orbit. Every day, our agencies create events. That wasn't so twenty years ago. Paradoxically, the rise of virtual media has led to real-life events happening in counterpoint.

Advertising meets street art. Graffiti artists paint walls or anything else they can find on the streets. They've found their own place to express themselves. Their own media. To expose their work, art galleries have to break down these walls. When Banksy paints a ladder on the separation wall between Israel and Palestine, when he writes the word "boring" on a gray project building somewhere, when JR installs his women's faces on the walls of a Rio favela, their art is political. These artists have made street art come of age. In their own way, they're practicing Media Arts.

Media Arts. It's like the expression was made for Absolut. Absolut brought art to the media. We have produced hundreds of advertisements for Absolut in twenty-five years. Most of them were designed with major artists, sometimes even by them. As early as 1985, Andy Warhol and Keith Haring were painting the label. Many established figures followed in their footsteps: Kenny Scharf, George Rodrigue, Paul Warhola.... Then Absolut became a major sponsor of the arts. The first sculpture in its campaign was commissioned from major French sculptor, Arman. The first series of fashion photographs were by Helmut Newton. The Absolut dress was made by David Cameron. Absolut has gone on to work with Jean-Paul Gaultier, Gianni Versace, Azzedine Alaia, Marc Jacobs, and many, many other designers.

Over the years, all this has turned into an Absolut collection. Absolut behaves like some eclectic and passionate art dealer. It has celebrated major names. It has discovered new talent. Our ads for Absolut have come to be recognized as art in their own right. They have been exhibited in museums the world over. Michel Roux is the man who made Absolut what it is. He fashioned its worldwide success. Asked about the ads, he said, "That's not advertising anymore. It's art."

Nissan

"We learn less from people who resemble us," said Carlos Ghosn that day in June 2008.

The CEO of the Renault-Nissan Alliance is truly a "citizen of the world," to quote from the title of a book he published a few years ago. The phrase evokes globalization—a source of anxiety to many Europeans. The tendency where I come from is to see globalization as a threat. People forget that globalization has also opened markets the world over to European businesses, and that it has been the main force behind the rise in living standards over the last twenty years. Detractors don't see the positive aspect that encourages people from all the over the world to mix, to develop relationships and mutually enrich each other's lives. They also undervalue the fact that thanks to the Internet, we can have instant access to virtually the whole world's knowledge base, and to artistic works.... Such were the issues we were discussing with Carlos Ghosn that day in June 2008. We had asked him to answer Rob Schwartz's questions in front of an audience of three hundred of our managers. Rob is our network chief creative officer. Their discussion was very broad, from car models, design, advertising, the Internet, globalization…to ethnic diversity.

To Rob's question on diversity, a question dear to Carlos Ghosn, he gave the following response: "It is a fact that reality is perceived mainly through differences. If there are no differences, there is no perception. You perceive different things because they are different. You perceive colors because they are different; you perceive shapes because they are different. The perception of human beings is through differences. Difference is at the base of diversity. Everything is based on diversity. Human beings practice diversity all the time without even seeing how important it is." He went on to apply these thoughts to the world of business, pointing out, "We know that diversity pays. But now there is another reality about diversity. It is that nobody likes diversity. We like commonality, we like people who look like us, speak like us, think like us, that's why we feel comfortable with it. The reality of the world is that you learn from diversity, but you are comforted by commonality."

In France, the term *diversité* has taken on a political or social connotation because it is used as an euphemism to describe citizens from an immigrant background. Internationally, the concept evokes the potential for wealth creation when companies start breaking down silo mentalities so people from different backgrounds with different skills can come together. "Make sure Japanese people don't just work with Japanese people, make sure engineers don't just work with engineers," says Carlos Ghosn.

In 1999, Renault bought 36 percent of Nissan. From that day on, the Japanese, as well as the French, enjoyed an even more diverse blend of cultures.

Equitable Alliance

Renault saved Nissan from bankruptcy. Under the circumstances, talk of takeover, acquisition—at any rate a merger—might have seemed appropriate. Carlos Ghosn banned such words from his vocabulary. He knew that saving both companies' individual cultures was crucial to long-term success. This really meant respecting Nissan's identity. It is why Carlos Ghosn rejected French attempts at hegemony so vigorously.

The structuring of the Renault-Nissan Alliance, as it is called, is unique. It may herald future forms of governance more in line with today's global needs. Each company has kept its independence, its shareholders and board. Strengths are pooled. Differences learned from. This is the intelligent way to change scale. The market demands it. Carmakers today need to establish worldwide presence, offer a full range of vehicle categories, and invest massively in ever-cleaner models. Mass-market manufacturers cannot survive unless all three goals are reached simultaneously. To do this, they need a critical mass, which is now much larger than it used to be. The Renault-Nissan Alliance has achieved this change of scale without the loss of identity.

Most people were skeptical at the outset. One French business weekly ran a headline saying, "What on Earth Is Renault Getting Into?" A motor magazine said, "The Alliance won't be posting profits in the next ten years." Others called it a bluff. The following year, in an incredible tour de force, Nissan made a 2.1 billion-dollar profit, up from a 5.9 billion-dollar loss the year before. As years went by, some labeled Carlos Ghosn's work just a cost-cutting effort on a scale never previously witnessed. Renault and Nissan's joint purchasing structure is currently running at 80 billion dollars per year. But it's not just about economies of scale. The crucial fact is that ten years of working toward a joint future has built a foundation of trust between the two corporations.

One day, I heard Carlos Ghosn say that the equilibrium between Renault and Nissan was protection against a hostile takeover. If a third car manufacturer entered the field and failed to respect the terms of the agreement that specify non-domination, the mainspring of what makes the Renault-Nissan Alliance work would be broken, proportionately destroying value created since 1999.

The Alliance not only moved into profit very rapidly but also established swift, strong sales growth—until the recession kicked in—making it the third largest car manufacturer in the world. Years later, Nissan and Renault became the first manufacturers to make electric cars for the mass market, getting a jump on competitors.

I have worked with both firms over the last ten years, but mainly with Nissan. You have to know at least one of them well to appreciate the subtle balance between

178

the Alliance's determination to protect each company's specific identity, and its eagerness for both entities to learn from each other. Over and above sharing platforms, engines, purchasing units, and quality control, both sides know just how far creating value means not intruding on each other's cultural specifics.

Sharing genuine respect for each partner's uniqueness makes a balanced partnership possible. At first, since Renault was providing the funds, the burden of proof lay with them. So Renault sent out plenty of signals. Two examples: whereas Daimler Chrysler, Nissan's other potential partner, had insisted that the prospective shareholder agreement should come under German law, Renault agreed to submit to Japanese legislation. Secondly: Carlos Ghosn announced that if Nissan's turnaround failed, both he and his entire executive committee would resign. That was the clincher: proof of a partner's commitment to shake up the entire enterprise while still respecting its traditions and values. That is how Nissan was able to recover.

Renault saved Nissan, but was careful not to behave as a savior. In this way, it reinforced the Alliance…. Time has passed. Since 1999, much has changed. Since then, Nissan's sales have enjoyed spectacular growth the world over, making Nissan one of the largest and most successful car manufacturers today, a reference in the industry. The horizon seems limitless for the leaders of the Yokohama company. And as a result, a new balance is subtly emerging within the Alliance. The driving forces inside the Alliance are evolving.

The Alliance faces many other challenges. I will not mention them all. But I would like to evoke just two of them. Two big issues: The first is to convince financial analysts that the thinking behind the Alliance is sound. The market tends to penalize the Alliance because it is an unfamiliar concept. There is nothing to compare it to. The other challenge is in redesigning governance to ensure that the Alliance survives its creator. A new way of functioning needs to be invented again.

Solving these issues, and others, is the condition that will enable the Alliance to be a model for the company of tomorrow. It will then be definitely seen as a pioneer, an agent in the spread of a positive and balanced form of globalization. And as such it will survive the test of time.

Shift

On September 2, 2004 in Tokyo, Carlos Ghosn launched six new models. During his speech that day, this is what he added: "'Shift' is a single word that captures the passion and commitment that have revived Nissan, and drive our future. Everything we touch, we shift; and everything we shift, we try to make better, and uniquely Nissan. And that deliberate shift in values touches everything at Nissan…. Shift is who we are, and how we work. It is a challenge to each employee, each supplier, every dealer to reexamine how they work, and how they can create more value for our customers."

A mere word, in this instance "shift," introduced through advertising, can sometimes establish itself as the clearest expression of what a brand stands for. Not surprising, since our role is to express the essence of brands as concisely as possible.

This was the mission Steve Jobs gave to our agency when he returned to Apple "from exile" in 1997. Lee Clow and his team created the "Think Different" film that clearly played a pivotal role in helping to bring Apple back to prominence. Introducing the film to an audience of IT distributors just a few days before its first airing, Steve Jobs said: "A lot of things have changed, the market's a totally different place than it was a decade ago, and Apple's totally different, and believe me the products and the distribution strategy, and the manufacturing are totally different, and we understand that. But values and core values, those things shouldn't change. The things that Apple believed in at its core are the same things that Apple really stands for today. And so, we wanted to find a way to communicate this, and what we have is something that I am very moved by. It honors those people who have changed the world. And the theme of the campaign is Think Different. It's the people honoring the people who think different, and who move this world forward. And it is what we are about, it touches the soul of this company."

Our mission is always to try to elevate the brands entrusted to us to a higher plane. This is our ultimate goal. There are many ways of describing the movement involved in propelling a brand upward.

We talk about vision. Other people refer to mission, ambition, reason for being, credo, motto, sense of purpose. Pepsi's *ambition* was previously to be the choice of a new generation. Apple's *vision* was freeing man from the constraints of machines. Body Shop is founded upon a *credo*, which is that a business can be built without compromise. Club Med's *reason for being* is to provide an antidote against modern life. Nissan speaks with one voice the world over thanks to its *motto*, "Shift," which is the same in every country. And Dove has given itself a *purpose*, which is to show women of all ages and all walks of life their intrinsic beauty.

From agency to agency, from one management consultancy to the next, the vocabulary may vary. Some will talk of a reason for being, another of vision, a third of purpose. Each may claim that these terms represent widely different, even incompatible approaches. Marketing experts will defend passionately their preference for one term to the exclusion of any other. Their stubbornness is narrow-minded. It deprives them of new insights, of original thoughts about the brands they must manage. If Pepsi, for instance, had defined itself in terms of a credo or a purpose, I do not believe it would have come up with "The Choice of the New Generation." Everything depends on how a subject is approached. For one brand, it may be more appropriate to talk of vision or ambition. For another, of credo or purpose. When imagining what the future could hold, you want to let the mind fly acrobatically from one option to the next. Personally, I attach very little importance to the manner in which a new angle is found. What matters is allowing a brand to move to a higher plane, however this happens.

The New Car

The most striking shift operated by Nissan so far has already cost it four billion dollars. That is the dramatic amount invested in electric cars. Or as Toshiyuki Shiga, Nissan's COO, puts it, in "the first all-electric car for the mass market." Betting on electric cars represents a fundamental shift for Nissan and Renault. It is a defining moment in their history. The Alliance is already the acknowledged leader in zero-carbon-emission vehicles. It intends to hold that position for the next decade. No emissions. No gas. No exhaust pipe. And for the driver, no noise, no smell, no vibrations.

For five years already, Carlos Ghosn has been predicting that electric cars would take 10 percent of the market by 2020. Many factors may occur to speed up that process, such as a new oil price hike. Ghosn's competitors do not agree. They predict electric cars will remain at 1–2 percent. They will tell anyone who wants to listen. But when Nissan launched its Leaf, the landscape suddenly shifted. The future started driving California freeways. Some people's conviction was shaken. The Boston Consulting Group published a prediction that electric cars would reach 7 percent by 2020. Whether they comprise 10 percent of the market by 2020 or later, clearly electric cars are going to succeed.

There are currently six hundred cars per thousand inhabitants in the Western world, meaning the US and Europe combined. That's compared to an average of fifty per thousand in emerging nations. Even if these countries settled in the coming years for half the number of cars we have—three hundred cars per thousand—the total number of cars releasing carbon dioxide into the atmosphere would still double. The planet just couldn't support that. Governments all around the world know this. When Prime Minister David Cameron of Great Britain introduced savage cuts in public expenditures last year, he decided to maintain a high level of subsidies for electric car manufacturers. "No dithering where new technology and the environment are concerned," he said.

At a purely political level, electric cars are welcome for at least two reasons. On the one hand, they create jobs. Carmakers suddenly need engineers from disciplines not previously involved in making them. Thousands of chemical engineers and specialist electricians will join them. So new technologies create long-term jobs. The other crucial goal politicians have set is deficit reduction, particularly with regard to their trade balances. Electric cars will substitute national and local energies such as solar power, nuclear power, or wind power, for imported oil. As Carlos Ghosn points out, "It matches the two priorities that I heard from the new majority in the House of Representatives."

On August 2, 2009, Nissan opened its new headquarters in Yokohama. A Shinto priest was invited to perform a blessing to ward off negative spirits. Then came the moment everyone was waiting for: the unveiling of the Nissan Leaf by Carlos Ghosn. This was the first time Nissan employees, reporters, and the general public were able to see the car. The event was

184

headline news on every TV station. I was in Yokohama that day. I knew this was history in the making. I knew Nissan would be remembered forever as the company that had brought the electric car to the masses. It will go down as a pioneer.

Major innovation, such as a zero-emission engine, brings about a chain reaction of change. The Leaf recycles energy from its braking system. There are applications to check battery levels, to heat or cool the interior by remotes using a mobile phone or a computer. One optional extra will offer a solar panel on the back spoiler to recharge a battery for car accessories. The car is so different, so absolutely new that in our launch film, we just called it "The New Car." Then there were films that showed a polar bear leaving a partly melted ice floe, traveling thousands of miles to thank the owner of an electric car by giving him an affectionate hug. And another film in which competitive cyclist Lance Armstrong, who has spent years riding behind cars that belch exhaust fumes, praises the fact that for the first time in his life he can cycle behind clean cars. No exhaust. The air stays clean.

Electric cars mean a lot will change, a lot will shift. The driver will have to get used to the one-hundred-mile range. Critics talk of "range anxiety." As it happens, 90 percent of Americans drive much less than one hundred miles a day. On average, they use their cars six times per day for trips of ten miles or less. Drivers will also have to get used to a new business model, similar to that of mobile phones. They will buy their vehicle and rent its battery, just as a person buying a phone device rents time by the minute. Drivers will need to learn to use high-speed public charging bays in major cities and along interstate highways. They will have to adopt a new way of driving. The experience is a very different one to driving a car equipped with an internal combustion engine. Electric cars are transmission-free. The accelerator sends energy straight to the engine. Nothing comes between the driver and the wheels. Driving becomes a totally different sensation.

The Nissan Leaf was voted Car of the Year in Europe, in Asia, and in the world. In April 2011, *Fast Company* ranked Nissan fourth on its list of the Fifty Most Innovative Companies, behind Apple, Twitter, and Facebook, but ahead of Google, IBM, Amazon, Nike, and Microsoft. No other carmaker made the list. When it was published, *Fast Company* interviewed Carlos Ghosn. The reporter asked about doubts expressed by some Nissan employees. Ghosn replied, "We had to explain why electric is huge for this industry. People need to feel the passion, vision, determination, and focus. I didn't say it was going to be easy. I said it would be a challenge—but if someone could do it, we could." In fact, as *Fast Company* puts it, Nissan's CEO has proved just how shortsighted the critics were. The electric car has given 350,000 Nissan employees a tremendous boost. They are proud and enthusiastic. Better still, the Leaf has refocused the brand. Brian Carolin, Nissan North America's senior vice-president of sales and marketing, is very clear: "The big prize for me is, 'How can I use the Leaf to build and improve the Nissan brand? The gift of the Leaf is that it gives precision to what we stand for. Now we have a message. We stand for innovation."

The Leaf aims to be competitively priced compared with conventional cars in its category. This will remain true for future Nissan and Renault electric car models. Government subsidies are currently needed to reduce consumer price, but in the future economies of scale will make electric cars genuinely competitive. Sales will have to reach five hundred thousand to one million per year. Such is the Alliance's goal. Indeed, Nissan has always stated that every single model, without exception, must be profitable. Carlos Ghosn puts it very clearly. He says, "The Leaf is going to be one of the most profitable products Nissan has ever made."

At the outset, many reporters and potential customers were unable to conceal their skepticism. That is no longer so. Grand visions are forceful when they initiate the changes that place them beyond doubt. Every passing day increases their credibility. Nissan's electric car is gradually becoming a symbol. It represents not only a major shift for an individual carmaker. It also represents a shift for the industry as a whole.

Above all, it is a sign that we are about to witness a major change in the way drivers behave. As Carlos Ghosn told the *International Herald Tribune*, "There's demand for other types of cars. It's not just either-or. But owners of electric cars will never buy another type of car again."

Online

"Silvio Berlusconi caught in the Web."

So read *Le Monde*'s website a few days after the head of the Italian government was defeated in local elections in Milan. Next came defeat in a national referendum on water and energy. The opposition achieved scores rarely seen in a democracy: 96 percent were against privatizing water; 94 percent were against a return to nuclear power generation.

The man who had used his control of the major TV channels to infiltrate every aspect of Italian society was defeated by the world of the Internet and social networks. Web users' comment and analysis on the issues at stake in the referendum flew thick and fast. Critical comparative data was published online. Video satires denouncing the party's outmoded ideas were posted. Yes, the Internet took Berlusconi, who had held a near monopoly of power for years and was used to his party's domination of the political system, by utter surprise. Suddenly, instructions from on high were no longer being obeyed. Alberto Contri, a political analyst, an expert in new media, put it this way: "Those two elections signaled the end of a world. Citizen Berlusconi's political and business empire was dead. What the web showed was plain: it showed the emperor had no clothes."

A few months later, the sovereign debt crisis stripped Berlusconi of the remnants of his credibility, forcing him to resign.

There are eighteen million Facebook members in Italy, nine hundred million worldwide. Facebook is often compared to a "sixth continent." Chris Cox, the number two at Facebook, has a business card that reads, "Engineer by day, sociologist by night." He spends his nights trying to understand the tsunami Facebook has created.

Facebook is intergenerational. My generation uses it to meet up with schoolmates last seen half a century ago. Most people over fifty, though, still feel like intruders when they venture onto Facebook. Hyper Island is a Swedish university famous for its training courses in the digital economy. Its professors invented a distinction that has been adopted by academics worldwide, between "digital natives" and "digital immigrants." The former are under twenty-five, were born and raised in the digital era. The latter live in a world that came into being after they were born. They will remain "immigrants" forever.

Scientists have shown that the brains of "digital natives" actually grow differently. At early age,

190

neuronal connections are established according to new protocols. Synaptic circuitry is configured in a new way. Thought is less linear, preferring a tree system structure. This reflects a capacity for thinking about several different things at the same time. It is a characteristic of minds used to multitasking.... Digital practice begins at an early age: it plays an important role in structuring thought. Joël de Rosnay, who runs the Cité des Sciences Museum in Paris, speaks of the "symbiotic man." He thinks the human species is mutating under the influence of computers.

We live in a world where the exponential is normal. There are more processors in an iPod than in the technologies used by NASA in 1969 to send Neil Armstrong, Michael Collins, and Buzz Aldrin to the moon. Data processing capacity keeps growing faster and faster. The *New York Times* says that by 2050, the same iPod will be able to compress thirty-two million books, seven hundred and fifty million newspaper articles and academic essays, twenty-five million songs, five hundred million images, five hundred thousand films, three million TV shows and documentaries, and one hundred billion web pages. Everything will turn virtual. Databases will devour everything. All that man has created and designed over thousands of years will be reduced to a succession of ones and zeros.

Painful Metamorphosis

The digital revolution is forcing industries, in particular service industries, to rethink. Few are enjoying the challenge. At first, some people in advertising tried to underplay the effects of change. Sure, Internet was a major new medium in that it was going to play the part that TV used to play, the way fifty years ago TV stole a part of radio's audience. They thought maybe 20 or 25 percent was going to go to Internet. As far as they were concerned, Internet was going to be just one more option in the range of available media. They were not yet able to imagine a medium that spawns hundreds of subsidiary media.

Time has passed. Today's realities have become inescapable. People in advertising are in the grip of a new anxiety: they're scared of missing out on the latest innovation, the latest technological leap. They need to keep up to date, need to spend their nights surfing the web in search of the latest must-know sites. They're "always on," on permanent technological watch. Their nights are long.

Advertising professionals are becoming like medical professors, scanning the *New England Journal of Medicine* or the *Lancet* for the latest scientific developments. They're like lawyers plowing over judicial reviews that publish developments in jurisprudence, or physicists searching erudite academic publications for new discoveries. Advertising has joined the list of expert professions where people live in fear of being left behind. Some of my colleagues are unused to this demanding discipline, to the new pressure, having lived under the belief that they were protected by their creativity. Now they need to know how to brief a software engineer or an app designer. They also need to understand how to mix and match databases, how to manage the successive stages in the e-commerce process, and more.... A degree of precision is required in a world that has grown more sophisticated and complex. We no longer just talk about advertising imagination, but about competence and analytic rigor.

In a previous chapter, I referred to 180 in Amsterdam, one of the agencies in our network, and run by Chris Mendola. Five years ago, following a request from Adidas, Chris "digitized" his agency. Adidas's new head of marketing was a young woman with a background in the Internet. She decided to put a halt to all expenditures in classic media. She asked 180 to compete for the Adidas account with a range of agencies that specialized in digital advertising, so-called "pure players." 180 won the pitch, but at a high price. Forty out of a total of one hundred and twenty staff had to be replaced. Despite the fact that, just a few years earlier, 180 had been voted "Best Young Agency in the World" at the Cannes Festival. The average age of its employees was just twenty-eight. But still, it had to lose one third of them to keep in tune with the times....

TBWA employs some twelve thousand people. Simple arithmetic led Chris to say, "Four to five thousand people will have to leave TBWA in the near future..." Actually, staff turnover in our industry is running at around 10–15 percent per year. So an agency renews half its personnel over a five-year period. The trouble is, neither TBWA nor any other network can afford to wait this long. So the process of change is bound to be painful. The expression "digital revolution" is no euphemism.

The Right Pace of Change

There is such a thing as the right pace of change. Timing is everything. Google, Facebook, and many others were preceded by similar ventures that failed because they appeared on the market too soon. Social networks, for instance, were actually invented in 1995 by Classmates, then revived in 1997 by *Fast Company*'s social network, which was called Company of Friends, and finally adopted in 2002 by Friendster, which has since failed. Facebook was set up at the right moment, in the right configuration: a 2003 version for Harvard alone, then in 2006 for the world at large.

In the digital world, the potential is so vast that supply often precedes demand. This is what caused the Internet bubble in the early 2000s. A disconnection between supply and demand led to the digital economy being overvalued. When the markets realized where demand really was—way behind supply—everything collapsed. We may well ask, in the microcosm of our profession, if we are not recreating our very own Internet bubble. What if consumers don't really need permanent geolocalization, or constant electronic code barring to live more happily? What if "liking" a brand on Facebook wasn't anything more than just a temporary snapshot, very far removed from what is called "engagement marketing"? What if the desire to establish a constant conversation between brands and their consumers is often too ambitious? Not all brands have the staying power. Some might do better with successive forays.

Digital technology has brought about an economic revolution. It has changed our profession profoundly. But we have not yet got the full measure of it. People in advertising and their clients are avid for a new source for growth without really mastering the consequences of the new forms of activity they have devised. The head of Millward Brown consultants compares advertising agencies' headlong race into new media with that "irrational exuberance" that led investors to place their confidence in incomprehensible financial instruments and thus inflate the bubble.

The digital world is overloaded already. There have never been so many ways of reaching consumers, yet it is proving harder and harder for brands to make meaningful contact with them. Brands need to think about their digital "ecosystem" more subtly. They need to achieve a better balance between entertainment, dialogue and service. The apostles of content are betting on entertainment. The apostles of social networking are betting on dialogue. But in the digital world, the future for brands is also in service. Which is why manufacturers are starting to think in terms of "added service." What added service does Nike or Pampers need to offer? On Nike's website, runners can compare their performance times with those of their real-life friends. Pampers has an app called "Hello Baby" that allows pregnant women to monitor their baby's growth day by day. The future of marketing is in service.

The true digital revolution has yet to happen. That will be when new technology comes to match the way we live, to make a natural fit with the way we are, and not the other way around. Reality and virtual reality will enter into a new alliance to create and offer new services. One example is Tesco's South Korean virtual supermarket, Home Plus: posters in the subway show products on shelves just like those in real stores, and printed with active QR codes. Users scan their orders from their phones, before hopping onto a train. Their order is delivered to their home that same evening. Koreans are now able to do their supermarket shopping in the subway.

This Korean initiative exemplifies what the future holds in store for us. Content created for mobile devices will give consumers the option of purchasing any kind of product, starting with packaged goods. And a research study carried by Forrester has revealed an important evolution in terms of consumer behavior: after a search on mobile devices, six dollars are spent offline for every dollar spent online. Our role in the future will therefore be to find all the possible ways to connect online content to sales.

The growth in interactive TV, in Augmented Reality and mobile money, will soon allow companies and brands to provide a genuine revolution in customer experience before, during, and after purchase. US shopper marketing experts call the new processes "digitail," a cross between "digital" and "retail." Already, your own refrigerator can identify shortages of your favorite brand and order replacements for you automatically.

196

Your refrigerator will e-mail you a confirmation slip showing the orders, and augmented reality glasses will allow you to read this e-mail on your windshield. The more we digitize our lives, the less the dividing line between reality and virtual reality will mean anything. There won't be a dividing line anymore.

The Weight of the Future

The Internet has proved that a new space can develop organically of its own accord, horizontally, through, and between those who invented it and breathe life into it every day. Millions of different initiatives, millions of different experiments have come to constantly consolidate this horizontal growth pattern. Nonetheless, there have been defining moments like Al Gore's White Paper of 1991 on the need to interconnect government services, hospitals, and schools. Twenty years later, a billion computers are interconnected, using the power of networking. In France, nearly one hundred thousand junior high school teachers exchange "best practices" and innovative teaching methods. The Internet encourages horizontal exchange. It multiplies communication exponentially. If France's centralized, domineering Ministry of Education can join the party, then the Internet can overcome any obstacle.

This new liberty has extended to business. Social networks in companies allow freedom of expression for all, without filter, without hierarchical control. Today's employees know what their bosses are thinking via

Facebook or Twitter. That's more efficient than a staff speech. Facebook gives human resources departments a new way to recruit. Individual creativity, individual personality is hard to assess in a job interview. It comes over clearly, sometimes too much so, on a prospective employee's Facebook "wall." Conversely, a candidate can learn more about a prospective employer through a corporate Facebook page and corporate tweeting than ever before. Prospective employer and prospective employee find themselves on an equal footing. Over time, social networks will become increasingly influential in the business environment. They will create new social bonds.

So the digital era will see a company's internal relationships remodeled. It will also accelerate scientific progress. The challenges ahead justify the statement that the future is weighing on the present. Current computer power is an indication of what lies ahead. Today's computers allow a level of simulation and modeling unimaginable only ten years ago. Green technology, genetic research, progress in nanotechnology, not to mention combining information sciences with life sciences, will all take arithmetic firepower. An exponential growth in data-processing capacity will be needed to confront the dangers and the potential of tomorrow's world. History is often marked by scientific invention that surfaces just when it's needed. Seen from this point of view, the Internet represents much more than an additional element in our everyday lives. It represents something mankind had to invent in order to survive. Its appearance was essential. History demanded it.

Edgar Morin, one of France's best-known philosophers, has said the main challenge facing us this century is developing our ability to build more bridges between branches of knowledge. Cross-fertilizing skills, making different forms of expertise work together, demands more than just one lab, one corporation, one nation. The bacteria, or rather the hybrid crossbreeding of two bacteria that launched an epidemic of food poisoning in the region of Hamburg, Germany, was identified within just a few days in a genetic engineering lab in China. Today's progress will be the result of an instantaneous exchange of global expertise such as only the Internet affords. Waiting two years for one's thesis to be selected by the mandarin academics of the *New England Journal of Medicine* is a thing of the past. Development in contemporary thought is now available in real time on the Internet. The Internet does not remove complexity. It tames it.

Horizontality, complexity, convergence are key words at the heart of today's realities. They mean different things, but all refer to things connected to one another. When a disciple expressed surprise at the range of his knowledge, Confucius said, "I do not possess great knowledge. I have simply found a thread."

Procter & Gamble

"Be patient," said Chief Executive Ed Artz.

I have encountered five successive Procter & Gamble chairmen. Ed Artz was the second of them. He may have been one of the most brilliant men to have run the Cincinnati-based company, a company that has nevertheless always tended to prefer informed discipline to flair.

Ed Artz took Procter & Gamble into the beauty sector. This was a turning point. Back in the 1980s, the company had made the move from household goods into skincare products. From Tide to Olay. Procter & Gamble was tired of having to fight trench warfare against rivals Unilever and Colgate to garner a couple of tenths of a point of market share to limited effect on profit. A couple of rows away in the same supermarkets where Procter's household goods were being sold, dozens of skin-care products were bringing in higher margins. Women are willing to pay more for a face cream than for a dishwashing liquid. They prefer to portray themselves as women who want

201

to look young and beautiful rather than hardworking housewives.... The mass market in consumer products has such heritage built into it. For the same amount of effort, one shelf will earn you more than another.

That day, Ed Artz was gazing at a bottle of perfume from a young fashion designer whose brand he had just bought. I spent a whole hour with him. Much to my surprise, we spoke only of skincare and fragrance. This was unexpected coming from the CEO of a corporation that had built its success on comparative campaigns and side-by-side demonstrations for detergents and scouring powders.

As I have said, we had just acquired the Wells Rich Greene agency in New York. WRG ran some major Procter & Gamble accounts, but only in the US. Their international presence was nonexistent. But we had agencies in some fifteen countries in Europe as well as Singapore and a few other Asian cities. Merging with a US agency was designed to bring our combined group credibility and critical mass. Our newly strengthened network, BDDP, was listed in the *Advertising Age* top fifteen worldwide for 1992. We thought that Pringles and Olay, two of the brands managed by Wells in the US, would soon choose to be represented by our network worldwide. This seemed natural. It was the reason we had bought the New York agency for such an astronomical price. As far as we were concerned, the opportunity to represent major international brands was priceless.

I told this to Ed Artz and his response was, "Be patient." Two seemingly inoffensive words that were a harbinger of things to come. Of course, Ed wanted us to show our mettle in New York. But I was fooling myself about this "Be patient" comment. To me, there could be no doubt that someday soon we would be working for Procter at a global level. So long as we could show we were up to speed in the US.... Well, we were more than up to speed. Over the next six or seven years, Procter & Gamble ranked us every year as one of their top two agencies. They conduct extremely detailed and careful annual assessments on their advertising agencies. Two years running, we came out on top. I could only become more confident. Sooner or later, I knew things would change. And sure enough, they did. But not as I had hoped. In fact, what happened was exactly the opposite of what we expected.

In 1997, several people in our New York office who worked on Procter & Gamble left us. Procter & Gamble's management took umbrage. There was a difficult meeting with our network managers. The timing was bad because Procter was undergoing a review of some of their agency relationships. In those days, they used three agencies locally in the US and four major networks at a global level. They decided to consolidate all their advertising budgets into their global networks, in order to have more weight within each of those networks. The result was they stopped working with their three local agencies, including Wells Rich Greene. We had invested hundreds of millions of dollars, some of which one might call personal funds, to be in a position to win Procter & Gamble's global accounts. We spent years learning to understand the company and build relationships. We had put a lot of energy into a goal that just evaporated. It was a fatal blow. We never recovered. The stubbornness with which we were determined to work for a company that was my very first client drove us into the wall.

I remember something Mark Twain once said: "It ain't what you don't know that gets you into trouble. It's what you know for sure that just ain't so."

Conflict Policy

I started out in this profession as assistant account executive on Ariel detergent in February 1971, just two years after it was launched. It was already the market leader in its sector. Forty years later, it still occupies that position.

An agency that works for Procter & Gamble cannot work for Unilever or Colgate. Such incompatibilities have led advertisers to spell out rules, published separately by each corporation under the title "Conflict Policy." This document comprises a large number of chapters because the different instances of conflict are so numerous. They are also increasingly complex because markets have come to overlap more and more. Conflict Policy has, I would say, fashioned BDDP from start to finish. At least, I can think of no other example of its influence being so profound. When we bought Wells Rich Greene, we had to resign contracts we had running with Colgate and Unilever in various European countries that represented some 10 percent of our revenue at the time. In the period when we were building our network, we had to set aside potential alliances with a number of brilliant independent agencies that worked for Procter & Gamble competitors. I remember that was a problem in Germany, Spain, and Holland. Acquisition opportunities kept drying up. In the end, we sometimes had to settle for partners that just weren't as good. Our growth slowed.

But then at other times, Conflict Policy was on our side. It stopped banks from selling us out to groups we were reluctant to join. For instance, we were able to prevent our new financial owners from selling us to WPP, who worked for Unilever. When Martin Sorrell, WPP's CEO, became very insistent, I had a letter delivered to him outlining client incompatibilities he would face if he took us over. And, I did not forget to suggest to Martin Sorrell that he forward our letter to every member of his board. We were able to avoid WPP.

Time passed. I went on traveling to Cincinnati to speak at conferences; I went on attending brainstorming sessions in Geneva. Then we became part of the TBWA network. Later Integer, the world leader in shopper marketing, and a major partner of Procter, joined us. More recently, on the advertising side, we won the Pur account in the US and Clairol Pro worldwide. That is a start. A small start. I am back where I started out in 1992: "Be patient."

Marketing School

I have always tried to understand where Procter & Gamble acquired its unique know-how. *Harvard Business Review* still calls P&G the number-one reference in marketing. I believe that achievement is rooted in the corporation's insistence on strict intellectual discipline. I know of no other enterprise that so rigorously sorts fact from opinion: every decision made has to be fact based, exclusively. This is something of an obsession. And of course, it has its problems. It leads people to behave as if everything not factual is nonexistent. Nonetheless, Procter is an amazing school of marketing where you always have to distinguish fact, to identify what is real in the magma of information one receives.

No company has ever had as much influence over the advertising profession as Procter & Gamble. Firstly because of the size of its advertising budgets—close to ten billion dollars per year. That makes P&G the largest advertiser in the world. Secondly because the need to optimize media investment has always led Procter & Gamble to seek a better understanding of the mechanics of advertising. They established the first mass-market brands more than one hundred thirty years ago. They invented Brand Management. They codified the principles of TV commercials. What matters are single-minded selling ideas, usually expressed in a thirty-second format. Procter & Gamble has identified various storytelling modes: testimonials, demonstrations, slices of life…. They played a large part in the blossoming of US media companies.

Today, they are endorsing the integration of all forms of communication across the board. They have set up a pioneering organization in this field. They are also leading the way through the Internet, with all their brands actively exploting the countless new opportunites it provides. Finally, perhaps more than any other company, Procter & Gamble has thought about how agencies should be paid.

In addition to all this, Procter & Gamble has recently taken a determined and highly unexpected creative turn. After years of stereotypical, conventional campaigns, they have understood that reality has shifted. If a message is not at least somewhat entertaining, it will be ignored and zapped. The old approach was repetitive advertising: what mattered was repeating the message as often as possible. Creativity used to be an optional extra. For thirty years, it was superfluous. Procter & Gamble took the view that it was often just too haphazard and uncertain. Not anymore. Now it is seen as compulsory. Today, Procter & Gamble, like many other companies, knows you need to seduce people, not just convince them. You need to entertain, not just sell.

Out of all the recent Procter & Gamble campaigns, the Old Spice campaign is perhaps the best example. It has become a cultural phenomenon. The expression, "Smell like a man, man" has been adopted and twisted in all the talk shows. The actor who embodies the essence of virility has become a star overnight. No advertising festival has escaped this campaign. Every jury has awarded it a major prize. Another great example is the film Procter & Gamble produced for the last Winter Olympics: before and after the competition, the nervous tension is palpable in athletes' faces, in the way they move, the way they concentrate, look down at the ground or up at the sky, the way they glare at rivals as they near the starting gate. All these images are intercut with shots of their moms looking anxious or proud. The film's strength lies in the fact that the athletes you see are not adults, but girls and boys aged eight to twelve, perfectly mimicking the attitudes and nervous tics of their elders. It is in fact a film in which children act like adult athletes in competition. After forty-five seconds of seeing them winning parallel slalom races, spinning twenty feet above the ground in acrobatic ski trials, flying four hundred feet through the air in a ski-jumping event, constantly watched by their moms, the film comes to its neat conclusion: "To their moms, they'll always be kids. P&G, proud sponsor of moms." International critics voted this commercial best corporate film at the Winter Olympics.

For a long time, creativity was a weapon used by small, local businesses, an alternative to the big multinational dollars. Their wit reinforced the notion that small is beautiful. But for nearly ten years now, Procter & Gamble has been leading a whole stream of large companies in its wake. Every year, *Creativity* magazine establishes a creativity ranking for advertisers. Nowadays, you see a fair number of big companies in the top ten. Ten years ago, you would never have seen Procter & Gamble on the podium. It is no longer true to say that size and creativity are incompatible.

Big is Beautiful

In 2008, at the Cannes Advertising Film Festival, tribute was paid to big corporations, and notably to Procter & Gamble, which was voted Advertiser of the Year. I was asked to make a speech to mark the occasion. In homage to the interest that Procter & Gamble is now showing toward creativity, I titled my speech—unoriginally, I have to admit—"The Beauty of Big."

In a way, Procter & Gamble is *the* multinational. It sells hundreds of brands, twenty-three of which, such as Pampers, Tide, Olay, or Crest, make more than one billion dollars in sales per year. The corporation has decided that its goal is to win one billion new customers in the next five years. That's quite something. It means finding five hundred thousand new customers every day.

When I decided to entitle my speech "The Beauty of Big," my aim was not just to celebrate Procter's newfound creativity, but above all to applaud the series of initiatives, most of them charitable, launched by the corporation in recent years. It's an impressive list. Procter & Gamble is distributing packets containing a product that turns ten liters of potentially lethal drinking water into clean water within seconds. Whenever anyone buys Pur water filter products in the US, such packets are given away in the field. Since 2004, Pur and its partners have distributed nearly two billion liters of drinking water. You need to see a young Procter executive demonstrating the effectiveness of

209

his packet in an African bazaar. He pours the stuff into a jerrican of stagnant water inhabited by all kinds of nasty things. When he offers his audience a glass of water, they usually ask him to be the one to start. Unable to refuse, he drinks it. Pretty brave.

Following Hurricane Katrina, Procter & Gamble launched its "Loads of Hope" operation with Tide. The idea was to provide free mobile Laundromat services to natural disaster victims. Trucks loaded with washing machines drove from one neighborhood to the next. The operation was repeated after the devastating earthquake in Japan in March 2011. With Always, Procter & Gamble has established a program to help young African girls to stay in school when they have their periods. With Olay, Procter & Gamble has also invested in skin cancer research. Unilever brands are no slackers in this field. Dove has started a program to battle anorexia, which makes sense given that it embodies the idea that all women are beautiful regardless of age or size. Most of these initiatives become famous because Procter & Gamble or Unilever operate on such a vast scale.... As for Pampers, it is handing out a tetanus vaccine for pregnant women in Africa, involving millions of vaccinations. This is a partnership with UNICEF that is said to have already saved tens of thousands of lives. A documentary film has been made showing nurses traveling up to ten miles on foot to vaccinate mothers in remote villages.

Such initiatives receive a mixed response. Some people see them as just a cynical gambit to sell more products. But mindsets are shifting. There has been an upheaval in attitudes. Everyone on earth is now aware of the problems of our time. The average mom would rather help hand out vaccines than receive a savings coupon or points in a loyalty program. Clearly, the bigger the company, the more business it does, the more injections it can provide to save lives. Charitable deeds are happening on a mass scale. That's what I meant by "Beauty of Big."

Large companies can have a lot more impact than they believe. Among the hundred largest economic entities in the world, forty-nine are nations, fifty-one are corporations. Not harnessing the wealth created by those corporations to help people in need would be insane. The urgency facing the world demands it.

In November 2010, I was asked to speak at a seminar in Cincinnati. The audience included three hundred senior managers from Procter & Gamble. I was happy to be there. Forty years in, I had come full circle. I spoke about Apple, Pedigree, Nissan, and Pepsi. I also spoke about Procter brands. And I concluded with these words: "The economic crisis we have just been through has not just damaged the reputations of major financial institutions. It has damaged business as a whole. Procter & Gamble is one of the rare companies that is acting to help people all over the world. You should feel responsible for letting people know the essential role companies like yours are playing. This is within your power. You can make six billion people see large corporations in a better light."

I hope the day will come when people recognize that corporations have a major role to play in confronting the social upheavals to come. Those social upheavals will be on an unprecedented scale. "Don't forget, only companies create wealth, which is the basis of any government social policy," a French government minister just recently exclaimed. Sounds pretty obvious. But sometimes the obvious is controversial, especially in the older nations of Europe. Companies have a part to play because they can help shift growth from a rate between 1 and 1.5 percent, which means social stagnation, to a rate between 2.5 and 3 percent, at which point redistribution of income can begin. Some facts are well known, often repeated, and finally ignored.

One growth point makes all the difference. Or nearly.

Quality

"Imagine if we were more afraid of mediocrity than we are of failure," exclaimed John Hunt one day.

From Shanghai to Sao Paulo, every art director and copywriter in the business knows John Hunt, who founded the most creative agency in South Africa, one of the best in the world. He trained many generations of creative people, spreading an obsession for quality. His disciples have fanned out into creative departments the world over, including New York. John Hunt is our network's international creative director. He's has never been soft on banality. In fact, he's fierce in that way. To him, pride in one's work, however old-fashioned that may sound, is the best motivation a person can have.

Every profession deserves respect. In reality, it's our inability to seek excellence in our chosen field, whatever that may be, rather than the nature of that field itself, that makes many of our lives seem dull and pointless. I believe that advertising, a much-derided profession, can be a wonderful way to earn one's living. And contrary to what people sometimes say,

213

the public image of advertising is not so eroded. In fact, the opposite is true. Twenty years ago, only car salesmen were lower down the scale of professional respect. Today it would seem that real estate agents, lawyers, and bankers have all slipped further down. If you include politicians, who tumbled down ages ago, that makes a substantial part of the working population that can no longer look down on us.

Like John Hunt, I've always tried to do my best at my job. I hope I've succeeded, but in the early days I was torn between two very different schools.

The Ladder

In the seventies, I was leading a kind of double life, creatively speaking. I had been trained by Procter & Gamble. I knew nearly all there was to know about that corporation's ways. I knew the importance attached to what were known as "selling ideas." I knew how much execution mattered, in other words, the precision with which an idea is conveyed. Will it be a testimonial? A demonstration? A before and after? Or a slice of life? Procter & Gamble had done such a comprehensive job classifying, analyzing, identifying, statistically dissecting the pros and cons of each of these formats that there was little room for any kind of creativity. You just couldn't step out of line. Very occasionally, we'd come up with a really good idea. When that happened, conventional and laborious execution ensured that no one ever noticed.

When I was a creative director, we'd reap a harvest of awards for other clients at the Cannes Advertising Festival every year. Our agency was among the two or three most-awarded agencies in France. Inside our creative department, staff working on the Procter & Gamble account stood apart from the rest, in a conceptual ghetto of their own. As for me, I found myself switching mindsets according to whether I was working on a Procter campaign or a campaign for one of our other clients. On the one hand, there was the stifling discipline. On the other, a yearning for innovation. TV advertising was only a few years old in those days. We were learning the tenets of a new craft. We made many mistakes. Our other clients were on our side. They forgave us when we went wrong. And the laws of probability ensured that sometimes the odd nugget of inspiration slipped through the net.

This schizophrenic life lasted for years. I aimed to be competent when acting for Procter & Gamble. I aimed to be creative when working for my other clients. But I didn't like the double life. I wanted to find some means of combining the two ways of thinking: just as physicists will always seek to reconcile opposing theories, I longed for some solution that would bring incompatible approaches into harmony.

One drizzly November evening in Normandy, in northern France, more than twenty years ago, I sketched out "the Ladder." On this ladder, I aligned what I thought was every possible mode of expressing what a brand means, does, and stands for. I found six such modes: awareness, attribute, benefit, territory,

value, role. Some brands just need an increase in
awareness: we had, for instance, helped a tiny licorice
candy brand from the remote southern area of French
Catalonia double its sales with a sexy three-second
TV commercial (there is such a thing as three-second
commercial on French TV). Some brands were able to
emphasize a specific *attribute*—like Avis, who pounded
away at the fact that they were number two to Hertz,
so had to try harder. An historic example that is still
relevant. A majority of brands, of course, were *benefit
oriented*: They liked to claim "Washes Whiter," "Kind
to Your Skin," and so on. This was the rule at Procter
& Gamble.

But many other registers were available to advertisers,
too. *Territory* was one: Ralph Lauren's campaigns,
for instance, with their classic New England appeal.
Promoting *values* was another, like Nike, who always
stressed the glory of doing your best. Yet another
might be emphasizing a brand's social *role*, like Apple,
with its emphasis on making computers accessible
to everyone.

The Ladder was a turning point. It showed the full
range of modes of expression at a glance—Procter &
Gamble's, as well as everyone else's. It showed what it
was we were creating and producing. It showed how
and why what we were doing worked. It offered new
modes of expression. It was like understanding your
coordinates on a map or in space. No tool has ever
been so useful to our network. I have seen "ladders"
on planners' desks around the planet. A tool invented
a few years before Disruption, "The Ladder" became

a vital part of Disruption. Should a brand give itself a role? Should it embody a value? Rely on a specific attribute? All this brought substance to our internal discussions. Questions creative talent had settled unconsciously in the past were now out in the open. Everyone could participate with a point of view. Everyone could contribute to the creative quality.

In those days, so long as people were watching their TVs, they could see our ads as frequently as needed. Now, people channel-hop. They don't see our ads as frequently as we'd like. Unless they actively want to see them. This is what's called instant engagement. If people like a film when they first see it, they post it on social networks or on YouTube. They'll stop and watch the next time they come across it on TV. They never get bored of it. On the contrary, they develop an appetite for it. I've viewed the Apple commercial with Einstein, Picasso, Gandhi, and Martin Luther King hundreds of times. Every time I see it, the pleasure is intact. Like with the best music videos. The Adidas film that shows Muhammad Ali apparently boxing against his daughter for real, being punched by her on the chin, explodes time barriers in a really joyful way. Whenever I show it at a conference, it provokes applause.... Until just recently, there was no correlation between impact and frequency of viewing. Now there is. Frequency of viewing is founded upon initial impact. It depends on it. The more you like an ad, the more you'll see it. This is a new relationship between quality and quantity. Quality creates quantity.

217

From Short Films to Proper Plots

Quality is about good ideas. It's also about production values and attention to detail. Some films, unfortunately only a minority, are genuine pieces of art. They are lovingly finished and honed. Of course, a spot can cost millions of dollars to produce and as much as three and a half million dollars for a thirty-second airing during the Super Bowl. Every second needs to be as good as it can. I have already spoken of the Mac vs. PC campaign in which two typecast actors play Apple and Microsoft. Mr. Mac is the stereotypical Apple fan. He's really cool. Mr. PC is not grossly caricatured. In fact, he's pretty friendly. But you can see he's all stiff and conventional. This is a campaign that went global. The only people who didn't get to see it were those who lived in countries, like the UK, where comparative advertising is not allowed. Everywhere else, though, those two actors became like stars in some popular TV series. We made more than fifty commercials with them. Quality of casting makes an enormous contribution to those films' strength. It gives them style. We auditioned some twelve hundred potential candidates for the parts. That's a record. Usually, you might see around forty. Which gives you an idea of the lengths to which Apple went to achieve a kind of perfection.

People remember the other Apple film I mentioned earlier. It ends with a dark-haired girl blinking. She appears after a long line of geniuses from the past, just before the signature motto, "Think Different." Our creative team in LA found this shot in a video archive. They used it to show Apple management what they wanted to achieve. The film was made. Dozens of girls were asked to blink before a camera in a casting session. None of them blinked as well as the little girl in the original footage. So we paid a lot in royalties to be able to use that shot. Apple doesn't compromise.

The Internet has changed the meaning of quality. Soon, some three-quarters of the communication material on the web will be video based. These videos will come in all different lengths. Not just that sacrosanct thirty-second TV spot anymore. The quality will lie in the storytelling. Skill in storytelling will make the difference.

Crispin Porter & Bogusky devised a campaign for Coca-Cola Zero, Coke's sugar-free brand, which proves just how vital storytelling is. It involved a film that showed brand managers at Coke taking furious offense at their colleagues at Zero for suggesting that Coca-Cola Zero tastes just as good as classic Coke. They sue! There are lawyers meetings between the two sides. Both hammer away at their arguments.... Here the quality does not lie in the skillful way in which a thirty-second spot is carved up into images, but in the accuracy with which the story is told. It lies in the credibility of the stormy, behind-closed-doors legal meetings that are featured.... Production quality is judged over time these days. Proper plots are going to mean more than meticulous storyboards.

Creative Director

Hollywood is the place to meet storytellers. The people at our LA office rub shoulders with them. Sometimes, they work with them. They enjoy being influenced by them. The environment is inspirational. We are fortunate that our biggest office is in California. California is intrinsically optimistic. It's a place where people are passionate about the future. Applied arts and future technology are on home ground there, from filmmaking to computer science, from the video-game business to advertising. I often go to LA. I can't say it is a city I love, but I have to admit it does have a certain vibe. It's different from New York: on the East Coast, you know you're in the eye of a business storm. In LA, you can reach out and touch a world in the making. In one of his recent books, highly regarded French economist Jacques Attali says LA is now the capital of the world, in the way that Bruges, Venice, Amsterdam, London, Boston, and New York all once were (and I guess Shanghai soon will be). According to him, LA took over from New York when Apple happened. This was around the time we made our Orwellian *1984* film about the Apple Mac. It remains a memorable date to us, the high point in the history of our office on Grosvenor Boulevard in Santa Monica.

I already talked about Lee Clow, the man who was behind that film. Lee is the heart and soul of our LA office, and the inspiration behind our network. I consider it a privilege to have worked with and for him. He is a living legend, one of the rare creative figures known around the world and one of the few whose reputation has spread beyond the field of advertising. Lee likes ideas. He believes that ideas lead the world. That they speed up change. He knows that advertising ideas can change a brand's direction. He believes their power cannot be underestimated. He can identify an idea before it has even happened, before it's ever been expressed. One or two words, or a rough visual are enough. Talented creative directors can detect tiny things and help make them big.

The philosopher Max Weber said great leaders combine legitimacy, competence, and charisma. I know of few jobs that demand these leadership qualities as much as that of creative director. You need to have created a large number of campaigns acknowledged by your peers. Legitimacy is founded on external as well as in-house reputation. Competence, the second quality you need, comes with time. It means helping creative people do their best, better than they ever thought they could do. Creative people who work for a great creative director are astonished to discover how good they can be. Finally, creative directors need to display Weber's third characteristic: charisma. They need to lead people who are very dissimilar in their anxieties: creative talent nervous that they might hit a block, as well as clients nervous about the risks they're going to be induced to take.

To great creative directors like Lee Clow in the US or John Hunt in South Africa, quality and creativity are inseparable. Apart from David Ogilvy, the founder of Ogilvy & Mather, they're all in agreement on that one. Ogilvy scorned the term "creativity." He thought it sounded superficial, a self-indulgent tic of creative people who liked to use it to promote themselves, regardless of the audience they were supposed to be addressing. Some people agree with him, including Denis Streiff, our network's CFO. His concern is maximum value for input. Recently he suggested switching terms. He suggested we drop "creativity" and use "innovation" instead. He claims "innovation" sounds more reassuring because it sounds more industrial. I believe the opposite. I prefer the warmth of the term "creative" to the coldness of the word "innovation." I prefer to think of L'Oréal or LVMH as being creative. And Danone and Nike, too. Creativity takes you one step further. Creativity, according to my dictionary, means "power of invention."

Our business has reached a turning point. It has recession to deal with. It has a digital revolution to deal with. These are painful, dangerous times. But I never miss an opportunity to remind everyone how lucky we are to be working in a creative profession at a time when economic growth is so utterly dependent on creativity. Twenty years ago, Tom Peters wrote one of the biggest business bestsellers of all time, *In Search of Excellence*. I don't like the word excellence much. I find it too conventional. And too pretentious. But I am very pleased to note that in the century ahead, creativity and excellence are bound to be synonymous.

Room 13

Rod Wright, who was our human resources director, believed our network should establish some sort of charitable action plan at a global level.

With a view to this, he wrote to the director of Room 13 suggesting a meeting. She replied that there was no time to lose. She was resigning within a few days—she was about to celebrate her thirteenth birthday. The rules stipulate that Room 13's chairperson must give up the job on his or her thirteenth birthday.

Room 13 uses artistic endeavors as a means of encouraging children's progress. It functions as a network of creative workshops based in elementary schools, always run by the kids themselves. The program was born in 1994, in a school at Caol, near Fort William, in a remote and impoverished part of the Highlands of Scotland. That year, children at this school asked their head teacher for a room in which to engage in unsupervised artistic activities. The head teacher allowed them permanent use of a room that happened to be numbered room 13. The students painted and sculpted there. They wrote stories and poems, all under the guidance of what would later come to be called an "artist in residence," an adult figure selected and paid for by them through money raised by selling their artworks. They divided management tasks among themselves. They had a chairperson, a managing director, a treasurer, a head of logistics and so on. Together, they took responsibility for day-to-day management, answering e-mails and invitations that came in from around the world. They also made sure that financial and planning tasks were performed as needed.

Today, nearly twenty years after the program was launched in Scotland, there are more than seventy Room 13s around the world. TBWA has accompanied a process of international expansion that is unique in its own way. First, we took the idea to South Africa, then to some twenty other nations. Each time, Room 13 sets up in a difficult neighborhood, where children have to deal with racketeering, vandalism, alcohol and drug abuse, and gang violence. Many are orphans, often because their parents had AIDS. In this cheerless context, these kids' everyday life is their primary source of inspiration. Their paintings and their stage plays speak of rape, incest, death, liquor, drugs, and… children's rights. Some of the work is arresting. It's *art brut*. You can tell the artist is often overwhelmed by his or her subject matter.

Children as Teachers

We discovered Room 13 in early 2004. In January of that year, Rod Wright saw a documentary about it on Britain's Channel Four TV. One hundred eighty students aged five to twelve attended that school. The movie revealed that they had won nearly every single school's arts festival prize the preceding year and that some of the kids' work had been exhibited at London's Tate Modern Gallery, among other places. Even more surprisingly, the children had directed the documentary themselves.

The idea seemed exportable, which is why Rod had found himself writing to Room 13's chairperson, whom, as I have indicated, was only twelve years old. She replied within the hour suggesting they take over the management of all Rod's projects for him! I have read this surprising missive several times over. It was precise and professionally written. Rod, along with Fiona Clancy, network head of Disruption, went up to see Room 13 in Fort William. What struck them was how mature the kids seemed. And how enthusiastic. Every single pupil spent between one and several hours a day in the workroom.

We took the program to South Africa first. We were told about a school at Botshabelo, a city five hours outside Johannesburg. The unemployment rate in the vicinity is around 70 percent. AIDS is at a record high. Despite this difficult context, the people at the Ministry of Education had nominated the school as the best kept in the district. A second workshop was opened at Soweto, the Johannesburg township. To launch these two programs, Rod flew to South Africa with two children from the management team at Caol. The Scots kids believed that their idea should be passed onto other kids. They wanted to meet their South African counterparts face-to-face. They wanted to explain how to set up a management team. They imagined that the management side of their adventure would be much harder to teach than the artistic side.

Our South African experiment proved that Room 13 was an idea that could be reproduced. However, the South African school system is very different to the Scottish school system. In South Africa, teaching is highly formal. Children are asked questions. They rise to their feet before answering. Then they sit down again. Kids adore school. They see it as a way of escaping poverty. A very different story to what happens in Scotland, where most kids see school as a waste of time.

The fact that Room 13 was entirely controlled by the children themselves came as a shock to South African educators. But those first two headmasters made it their business to see that South Africa's first two Room 13 projects were a success. Success breeds success. There are some twenty-seven Room 13 projects in South Africa today. Several thousand students attend daily. In the meantime, TBWA has helped start Room 13 projects in Katmandu, Bombay, Shanghai, Toronto, and Istanbul, as well as LA and Paris. California's Room 13 is located in South Central, LA, a neighborhood known for being chronically dangerous. During the first week, we showed students a DVD about Room 13. They were astonished to see that Scottish kids rap. People in Scotland had found inspiration in what young Americans were doing. Now, young Americans were going to follow in the footsteps of young Scottish kids.... Life is tough in South Central. It would hardly have been surprising if the funds raised by those children with their first exhibit had been spent locally. They weren't: they were sent to Africa, to help other kids like them, only even worse off, access drinking water.

Right from their first visit to Caol, Rod and Fiona realized that two factors had been crucial to Room 13's success. The first was having an artist in residence, an adult able to coach and guide kids. The second was that Room 13 must not be a burden on its host-school's budget. Those two conditions have been respected at the seventy-plus Room 13 projects established globally. Neither the artist in residence, nor the cost of equipment, nor travel costs, nor any other costs are billed to the school. The kids deal with all that themselves.

The artist in residence—we say AiR—is paid for by the children. Sometimes we help select him or her. The candidate must be neither a teacher nor a parent nor a social worker. Just an adult the children trust, who can provide them with self-confidence and a sense of discipline. The artist in residence is not there to turn the kids into professional artists, though that can happen. He or she is there to help them grow up and blossom through art. He or she never tells children what to do. Rather than say a picture is beautiful, he or

227

she will ask the children to explain what it's about.... Choosing the right artist in residence is a crucial step in the process of setting up a new Room 13 project. They must belong to that rare breed of people who are generous and patient and able to step back and let children have their way. They need to be some combination of artist, thinker, and coach. Apart from which, as well as giving their time to the kids and their workspace, they have to make a living through art.

Annual shows are arranged in cities where Room 13 has been established. As well as the show at London's Tate Gallery, there have been exhibits at museums of modern art in Stockholm, Dublin, Johannesburg, and Edinburgh, as well as at London's prestigious Royal College of Art. Sir Nicholas Serota, director of the Tate Gallery, has called Room 13 "the most inspiring model for art teaching in the United Kingdom."

All Room 13s are self-funded. The annual cost varies, according to country, from several thousand dollars to a few tens of thousands. The workshops are not able to raise sufficient financing in their first year, but within two or three years they do. One of TBWA's roles is to help Room 13 projects survive that first year, but we don't hand out checks. We help find sponsors, we organize art shows, we design websites to put some of the work on sale. We also try to raise matching funds from public sources. In Canada, the City of Toronto has given Room 13 an annual endowment of twenty thousand dollars. In South Africa, since winning a Best Youth Sponsorship award, Room 13 has been given charitable status. Every time money is found, the

Mandela Children's Fund matches it rand for rand. This is a virtuous circle.

Many people at TBWA have become personally involved. Two of our London staff drove a Nissan Micra to Mongolia to help make Room 13 better known. Their route took them through Europe, the Ukraine, and Russia. Their vehicle was painted in Room 13's colors and carried the logo. They were exhausted by the time they reached Ulan Bator, but they still found the resources to sell the car at auction and hand over the sale price to street kids there. We are setting up a new Room 13 project in Mongolia now.

From Art to Expression

Emmanuel André, our network COO, is passionate about photography. He spent a week of his vacation giving photography workshops in South Africa. He visited the two schools in Soweto and in Botshabelo and photographed each of the Room 13 students there. He then decided that the students should photograph one another. Some of these pictures were so striking that Emmanuel decided to make a book called *Sharp*, sales of which brought in no less than forty thousand dollars. This provided funding for new workshops in South Africa as well as our first workshop in Hong Kong. Now, Emmanuel's done it again. Only this time he's raised more than one hundred thousand dollars. He made a new set of photographs in South Africa and shot a documentary movie, too. He organized an exhibit at a gallery in Manhattan's Chelsea district whose owner is considered to be the world's best expert on Keith Haring and Basquiat. A DVD has been issued containing the film about Room 13 and a film about the exhibit. Finally, Emmanuel has designed what he calls "Exhibition in a Box." This is a tool that combines flyers, catalogues, and reproductions of photographs so that every TBWA office can organize its own show to sell the photographs. Among other benefits, "Exhibition in a Box" ensures that works of art made in Bombay or Johannesburg sell in New York and London at considerably higher prices than they would at home.

The first Room 13 in France opened in September 2010 in a city called Villetaneuse, really a cluster of low-income neighborhoods on the outskirts of Paris. We had to face a counteroffensive by fine art teachers who said they were horrified that such an irresponsible project might ever be envisaged. It took us more than a year to convince the teaching body and local academic authorities to let us launch the program. Eventually, the authorities agreed to let students raise funds for their work. In December 2010, I attended the official opening, only to discover the main avenue leading to this suburban city is still called Avenue Lenin, a name not uncommon in what was once known as Paris's Red Belt.

The artist in residence at Villetaneuse had this to say about the work the children there produce: "Behind every piece lies the story of a mother, a cousin, a sister, a cat. Often the stories are sad…. It is not for us to tell the stories to you. The kids will tell you if they want to."

I spoke with some of the students in Room 13 at Villetaneuse. They told me about their work. I realized that by freeing up their creativity, we were also freeing up their ability to speak. This observation from the outskirts of Paris matched something that a schoolteacher in South Africa had already observed: "Room 13 kids talk in paragraphs, no longer in monosyllables." Somehow, you don't expect art workshops to improve speech. Room 13 does this because it doesn't just help kids create. It helps them organize. They become entrepreneurs. They rapidly acquire a sense of responsibility. They seem more mature than other kids. Many kids who come to Room 13 have checkered school careers. Room 13 helps them get back on track and feel more confident about their schoolwork.

Today, Rod Wright is sadly no longer with us. I want to pay tribute to his achievement. A few months before his death, he spoke with kids at Room 13 in Scotland. He told them about Disruption. The children responded with the thought that they, too, were "Disrupters." He told them how a network like TBWA functions. Well now Room 13 has grown into an international network of its own. The new chairperson at Caol, Lucy MacGillivray, had just turned eleven when Rod gave his talk. She summed it up in these terms: "TBWA is really just Room 13 for grown-ups, isn't it?"

231

Society

"It is totally shortsighted to believe that the purpose of advertising is merely to sell products. It can play a so much larger role in our lives." This is what Philippe Michel constantly reminded us. He was a man who truly left his mark on the advertising industry.

He repeated this statement shortly before the 1989 European elections. The polls were telling us that abstention rates were likely to reach frightening proportions. We were both worried about the withering of the idea of Europe. Philippe's dream was that two advertising agencies should be given the task of devising two impressive and contradictory campaigns to enlighten the younger generation on the issues at stake. He wanted to make sure there would be broad public debate, even if that meant being provocative. He felt that if journalists were unable to stimulate interest in such a crucial subject, then maybe advertising's more synthetic delivery would make it happen.

Philippe's dream was utopian. He believed that advertising was about more than just commerce. He

233

thought advertising had a know-how and a specific language that could be harnessed to any matter of public interest, whether the public was interested in it or not.

In the early seventies, shortly after the Cultural Revolution, Philippe Michel traveled around China. He acquired a taste for Chinese wall poster newspapers, or *dazibao*s. He dreamed of generating public debate on a gigantic scale through the use of all kinds of posters. These would appear on walls in public spaces as giant, photographically illustrated dazibaos. He thought this would encourage a democracy of the word, in which a plurality of contradictory views might be exposed to the free judgment of all.

Noble Causes

This is how Philippe Michel came to design an image that remains famous in France to this day: the so-called "baby" poster. This showed the words "Do I look like a government measure?" over the face of a newborn child. It was published just as French National Assembly representatives were debating government grants for abortion. It was intended as a denunciation of those people who were speaking too one-sidedly of the death of an unborn child. The idea was to remind them that there was such a thing as a life-loving approach to childbearing....

Not long after this, Philippe produced an ad in which he correlated quotations from sacred books. The

234

words read, "It's in the Bible and it's in the Koran." By underlining what sacred books have in common, he wanted to make a contribution, however minute, to an unlikely rapprochement in the Middle East....

A few weeks before the 1988 presidential elections in France, Philippe sent both main candidates, Jacques Chirac and François Mitterrand, a project for a poster that asked, "What will you do for people who will never vote for you?" This referred to multiple-handicap patients who were being expelled from public hospitals at the time because there was a lack of equipment to help care for them. In order to make sure he got a firm political commitment, every week Philippe sent the candidates an ad from a campaign he had devised. One poster he sent Mitterrand read, "François Mitterrand is expelling me from my hospital in six weeks." Then the following week, "in five weeks..." And so on. A similar series of ads was sent to Jacques Chirac featuring his name. The outgoing president, François Mitterrand didn't wait for the election to act. He signed a decree reversing the decision to expel handicapped people from public hospitals. The necessary funds were raised. Handicapped children in particular were not sent back to their parents. This was a fine example of how an advertising message sometimes doesn't even need to go public to be effective.

These few examples show that advertising is indeed all about effectiveness. It is a form of writing that is concise and compact. It has been refined and perfected over decades. It can be made to serve noble causes. It can bring issues of public interest into the limelight. Our agency has designed campaigns on all sorts of different social issues: on the fight against drug abuse, illiteracy, domestic violence; on the struggle for road safety, against AIDS, in favor of the environment. We made the longest-ever video chain so millions of Internet users could protest against nuclear testing. For Reporters Without Borders, a French freedom-of-the-press NGO, we hung photographs of oppressed reporters behind the bars of government-office windows and behind railings in big cities. You could see journalists behind bars on every street corner. We also made posters for a campaign against poor housing conditions that showed top-down photographs of families packed into a single room. These posters are life-size—just a few square feet across in the case of a bus shelter. The point of the campaign was to illustrate in a flash what it is like for thousands of people to be living crammed into tiny spaces.... We built a campaign called "Zizi Graffiti" around an animated clip that went global and became a YouTube favorite within days. It was designed to encourage young French people and people around the world to use a condom.

Excel, one of the agencies in our network, is France's number-one charity fundraiser. It counts a wide range of French and international charities among its clients, from Doctors of the World to Handicap International, the AIDS charity Act Up, and the Red Cross. Excel has raised more than a billion-and-a-half euros in its time. That's money well raised....

236

So, like many other people, we're doing our bit to try and make this world a better place through encouraging greater solidarity. Private corporations have been doing that for a long time. In the nineteenth century, they used to set up what were called "philanthropic" or "charitable" trusts. Today, corporations know that helping the world is an important part of what they do. No one can opt out.

Private Funding Supports Public Funding

Pepsi is a good example. In 2010, we recommended that they set up a new kind of very large-scale interactive charitable project called "The Pepsi Refresh Project." The idea was to encourage Internet users to vote each month for projects recommended by other Internet users. Pepsi would fund the winners.

The Internet's potential has rarely been tested on such a grand scale. One hundred and fourteen million Americans declared an interest in the program. That's more than one in three. The tally on refresheverything. com reached seventy-three million votes. That's more than the last US presidential election. One hundred eighty-three thousand ideas were put forward. Internet users chose hundreds to be supported. Pepsi contributed to the two winning projects two hundred and fifty thousand dollars each month. It gave each of ten runners-up fifty thousand. Then it made provisions for donations to be paid out to an additional twenty projects monthly. The total cost to Pepsi over one year was fifteen million dollars.

The Pepsi Refresh Project has supplied funds for abandoned children's homes and schools, for theaters and historical buildings in need of renovation. It has provided funds for bike lanes and playgrounds and baseball fields and sports centers and gyms in need of building. It has funded food banks. It has paid for animal shelters. It has supported programs to help develop children's creative potential in deprived areas; to fight illiteracy and school drop-out rates; to bridge the gap between generations. All these projects, big and small, taken together make for better everyday living. Pepsi is in tune with the times. Nobody believes much in spectacular global initiatives anymore. No one believes in magic bullets. But people do have faith in the combined effect of millions of individuals doing good stuff, in change by tiny touches.

Pepsi's campaign is a preview of what is to come. Private and public interests are converging to improve life for people wherever they are. Of course, most companies' resources cannot be compared to those of the government. Even when they act on a large scale. Even when they promote giant programs involving tens of millions of dollars, as in Pepsi's case, there is a limit to what corporations can do. All the same, thousands of corporations now feel they have a public role to play. The aggregate effort makes a real difference. That is why many people have come to realize that the private sector can and must support public sector initiatives.

Someone from Procter & Gamble in France once asked Jim Stengel, "How come Procter & Gamble employees do all this amazing charitable stuff at night and on weekends. And then they have to leave their positive energy at home when they go to work? What would happen if the brands they work on stepped in to reinforce the good energy? The impact of individual deeds would increase a hundredfold." Jim Stengel admits that this exchange acted on him like a wake-up call. It proved a turning point. Today, Procter hands out vaccines, helps purify water, cleans up cities, builds schools, and fights hunger. Procter & Gamble employees no longer need to feel that their life is torn between a socially aware part and a professional part. The two parts go together.

Triple Bottom Line

What Pepsi and Procter are doing belongs to an underlying trend that has been on the rise for over twenty years now. This is the growth in awareness of Corporate Social Responsibility. People judge corporations now on what has come to be known as the "triple bottom line": economic power, environmental impact, and social effect. Everything a corporation achieves in one of these fields reinforces everything it does in another of those fields. A new virtuous circle is in place. Greater respect for the environment and taking the public good into account heighten corporate presence. They increase a corporation's impact and thus its chances of succeeding at a commercial level.

Emmanuel Faber, managing director at Danone, confirms this: "In a large, quoted corporation, none of the shareholders has ever taken as much personal risk on behalf of the company as every single employee does. None has borrowed against salary, has built a house beside the plant, has raised his or her kids in the city or district where the factory is located. Consequently, our responsibility towards employees is greater than that towards shareholders. That is the truth. It's undeniable. The same is true of suppliers, subcontractors, and ultimately customers who, by (more or less freely) opting for a company's products, seal its fate. People like to pit social priorities against economic priorities, but the truth is that they are both aspects of the one reality. The line that divides them runs through the heart of our subjective perception. And nowhere else."

Companies like Procter & Gamble and Unilever have found a new place to express their awareness of their social responsibility. These corporations are seeking ways of making low-cost household goods that even the poorest people on earth can afford. That's one-fifth of the population of this planet. We're not talking about selling goods for a dollar here. We're talking about selling goods that cost ten cents. What these corporations want to do is to bring that part of the world's population that is excluded from consumer society into it. This is in their long-term sales interest. In this instance, "doing good" and "doing well" are synonymous.

The current economic crisis means changing our relationship to work, money, and consumption. It is making corporations reassess the way they function in a new context. Everyone knows we are entering a new age, one where the economy will be founded on values of moderation and civic responsibility. This will result in growth that will be more reasoned. We are entering into a new economic era in which, for instance, the cost of eliminating or recycling a product will be included in its initial purchase price.

If people in India, in China, in Brazil begin consuming as much as Americans do, the earth's resources will need to increase fivefold. We all know how crucial it is that new industries are pollution-free, that old industries improve their ecological impact. In fact, we need to go further than this. We need to reverse the logic and set up industries that actually manufacture a reduction in pollution. This is what is called "industrial ecology," a concept invented by a Swiss engineer, Suren Erkman, who said, "Ecology and industry, business and the environment must and shall join forces." There are plenty of examples, he says, such as the Ford factory in the US, with a roof that absorbs CO_2 and generates oxygen. Industrial ecology sounds like an oxymoron. It's actually a definition of a radical disruption waiting to happen.

It is not just the environment that is forcing us to reconsider everything, the same is true of other social issues. For example, to be able to sell household goods for merely ten cents apiece involves reassessing everything, from product concept development to manufacturing. In the same way, planning for a socially friendly future cannot mean just extrapolating the past along preset development curves. There has to be disruption, a break with former practices. The authorities are in a corner here. They cannot promote reforms for radical change. All they are able do is inch forward incrementally. They take measures like pushing our legal retirement date back by two years, or add a couple of percentage points onto the tax we pay. Politics will have to finally confront something I've long criticized in marketing: a lack of productivity caused by edging forward only with small steps.

There is a need to take measures that may seem irresponsible at first sight. Consider this example: How do we preserve the fabric of our economy? New forms of trade protection could be found that are not protectionist. The goal is not so much to preserve companies in one country but rather to support companies that behave in a civically responsible way, not just in their country of origin, but in all the markets where they are present. Examples of such companies in France, for instance, might include McDonald's, which has signed a unique farmers' charter. Or Toyota, which has built model factories in failing industrial districts in the north of the country.

Every corporation should be assessed in terms of its "triple bottom line." Every corporation needs to include civic and environmental contributions on its balance sheet. Dow Jones's "Sustainability Index" was established in 1999. It provides information to investors who believe that sustainability represents an important element in corporate performance. Right from the start, some 250 corporate players, including General Electric, Toyota, Procter & Gamble, and Unilever, were able to qualify. Qualification means providing detailed responses to a questionnaire that attaches as much importance to a company's civic and environmental performance as to its financial returns. A Zurich-based ratings agency analyzes the responses and establishes an annual corporate ranking. The number of qualifying companies is on the rise. European stock exchanges may soon come together to establish a similar index, using the European Union's criteria and weightings.

It seems inevitable that some time soon, a distinction will be made between companies that make a real contribution to the common good and those that don't. Those that create jobs and protect the environment as opposed to those that feel no compulsion to do so. Those that show greater civic responsibility should receive fiscal encouragement. Not all companies should be treated in the same manner.

I would like to believe that my country will be among those that show the way. Some people may complain that France cannot act in isolation without harming its vital interests. In that case, the answer is that the European Union must work as a catalyst. It will do so on one condition: that the authorities understand that if they want to promote truly innovative measures, they must not seek to impose them unilaterally on member states. They will have to build ad-hoc majorities for each successive measure. This is akin to so-called "majorities of ideas" in parliamentary politics, where people of differing political backgrounds coalesce on a one-off basis to push through a specific idea. If Europe were to work like this, it would engage in a virtuous process of what could be called "à la carte harmonization," whereby individual nations progress at different speeds. It would be more flexible. It would be less bureaucratic and more readily innovative. Any measure that has proved its worth in a handful of member states would gradually come to be adopted by others. In this way, the European Union as a whole would steadily move toward greater social cohesion.

Things still remain overcompartmentalized. But today's world is all about interdependence and interconnectedness. The solutions to our problems cannot be found individually, they must be plural. We need innovative forms of protection; incentive-based fiscal policies; and for the Europeans, a much more flexible way of moving forward. Meaningful reforms will prove effective only if they are interwoven.

Transparency

"Everything's different. Everything's the same."

The head of our Paris office, Guillaume Pannaud, was talking about the manner in which Publicis and Havas dominate the French market. As it happens, in world terms, TBWA has a bigger network than Publicis or Havas. In France, where it ranks third in size, it's nipping at their heels. But the perception remains that we sit squeezed out by the two homegrown mammoths. Their dominance is hardly new. When I first went into advertising, Publicis and Havas's hold on the market seemed even more dominant than it does now.

Back in those days, Havas was state owned. People rightly assumed that its chief executive must be at the heart of a political network that gave the firm its dominant status. Running Havas was a plum job, usually offered to some senior public official. One of the quirks in the French advertising environment was that the largest agency group was also a media broker, meaning it employed ad-space salesmen for major magazines and newspapers. To compound things,

Havas was an important shareholder itself in several media groups and owned, for instance, a national billboard network. This gave it a position of power across the board such as existed in no other major industrialized country. It was frustrating for the rest of us to see how Havas built personal relationships with our clients, who were compelled to buy space through its near-monopolistic sales operations. We were certainly fed up with seeing our own clients being offered luxury trips by media operators to far-flung destinations.

To a somewhat lesser degree, Publicis also combined consultancy, ad-space sales, and media management activity. People in the business used to call Publicis the "Ministry of Information, Number Two." Publicis's founder and his successor were notorious for the networking and lobbying skills that made their firm a worthy rival to Havas.

A decade or two passed. New French groups came to occupy the scene, including ours. Most of us in the business felt certain that, sooner or later, the Big Two's dominance would inevitably crumble. The newcomers had high professional standards. These would cast a shadow over the uneven performance of the old advertising "establishment." The latter may have had social connections, but the former had imagination. To each their own strengths and weaknesses.

Twenty years in, the old French political networks are still just as influential: less visible but no less important. In just one respect, there has been a quintessential shift: Havas and Publicis have caught up with the times: they have acquired new know-how; they have acquired creativity. And thus, because they've also managed to preserve their political ties, despite the passage of time, they remain center stage. Somehow, I feel I'm back where I started.

Past Battles

Everything's different now. Everything's the same. God knows we fought for change. We fought in two different fields. First, we wanted to see an end to a practice known as "opaque commissioning," meaning the sweetheart deals the media brokers gave agencies in secret to favor their media. Secondly, we wanted to denounce what we thought of as a closed shop.

I recently reread press cuttings from that era. Here are a few revealing extracts to show what we said and wrote on those contentious issues: "Independent companies such as ours that have been able to make headway, despite the punishing lack of transparency in our business, never forget that the prime mover behind this lack of transparency is a company that was until recently majority-owned by the State…" Elsewhere, we commented, "One could call this a closed shop whose influence undermines fair trade. Such, in any case, is the view of most advertising professionals. The problem is not just the high level of these groups' shareholdings in media corporations. It is more particularly the control they exercise through the distorting effects of cross-ownership." One influential competitor in the advertising business went so far as to say that he had "allowed us to succeed." This position was truly astonishing to me: a major rival boasting that he had power of life and death over us.

During this period, to the considerable annoyance of our competitors, we valiantly tried to shake things up. On occasion, we were woken up by agitated if not to say threatening phone calls in the middle of the night. We were precursors. We were shaking the establishment. We believed in transparency, and transparency was an underestimated virtue to some.

My partner Jean-Claude Boulet's position, as well as mine, was often criticized. We were accused of playing sheriff. Of being too moralizing. But we were nothing of the sort. Our decision to be transparent on matters of money had nothing to do with morality. The fact is that from day one we wanted to enter the big league. In order to achieve that, we had to act differently from the establishment. We needed to stand out from the crowd. We decided to hit them where it hurt.

Conflicts of Interest

In June 2011, a French magazine called *Stratégies* ran a headline about Havas that read, "Advertising, media consultancy, brokerage, sales and media, a vertically integrated Group." The critical article was about the consequences of cross-share ownerships. It alluded to internal directives and guidelines issued by Havas, on who to work with and who not to work with. The

Advertisers' Union spoke of an "essential neutrality under threat." The writer concluded that this "unusual situation" was probably unique in the Western world.

The dominant French groups argue that cross-ownership does not generate undue influence. But the remark calls for further analysis. The only guarantee that there will be no conflict of interest between advertising agencies and media groups belonging to a same holding would be a Chinese wall between them. This is the heart of the matter. Management can never vouch that employees will not cross the yellow line. The plain truth is that potential conflict of interest is already conflict of interest.

So how come this situation does not seem to shock everyone in France? Is this because of a legacy of vested interest that is obstructing this country's progress? Or the fact that chief executives see conflict of interest as normal? Or that the nation's leaders, especially those in government, actively try to accumulate overlapping responsibilities? It's as if this is just how things are done.

One sector more than any other seems to allow such practices to blossom, and that is the world of finance. It's not just that most bankers fail to avoid conflicts of interest. They actively seek them out. The head of Lazard Bank in Paris, Mathieu Pigasse, sees this on a daily basis. This is how he puts it: "Banking involves a whole set of different jobs. This can be a problem. Some of those jobs seem to stand in opposition to some others. There are many conflicts of interest." Pigasse is critical of a large number of practices, including one that appears to come as second nature to many bankers today: "There is a conflict of interest between those who fund or advise a company and those who recommend that same company to outside investors."

The thinking has grown so distorted that these contradictions have become an integral part of our economic environment. They have come to seem, well, just natural. France is peculiar in that a conflict of interest has to be manifest before a legal case can be made against it. In many other countries, the state of being merely in a potential conflict is liable to prosecution. As a result, my country's reputation is less than spotless. Transparency International ranks France twenty-fifth in its watchdog league. Twelve European countries are ahead of it. (And the United States occupied the twenty-fourth position....)

Returning to our French agency and the influence it was able to exert over the French advertising profession back then, I'd say it turned out in the end to be minimal. Despite the epic battles, we learned you cannot move mountains alone. We started out naïve and ended up lucid. The battles were noble battles. They may not have changed the world, but they did leave their mark on our company.

A few years ago, we organized a meeting of our European managers in Istanbul. The first night, the heads of thirty-two different offices met for a cruise on the Bosporus. At one point I asked Cem Topcuoglu, the head of our Turkish office, why he had not yet set up an event marketing agency. He replied, "I'll be able to do that soon because I'm finding a way of doing it that is transparent and clean. Until recently, that was unthinkable…" Five minutes later, I was talking to Mitja Milavec, president of our Slovenian office and Adriatic network. The Slovenian office's income was rising faster than the income of our other offices in the region. When I asked why, Mitja explained that there were two different working practices in the markets of former Yugoslavia: "Above the board and below. We work the first way and only the first way. Our refusal to do deals is holding us back in some places." Within five minutes of each other, two senior executives in our network had emphasized their insistence on working transparently, even though they were operating in countries whose modes of behavior are hardly considered exemplary.

My mind often returns to the happy coincidence of these two statements. It's one of my favorite memories. At least a principle that lay at the heart of what we were trying to do when we founded our agency had survived as an important element despite our being bought, taken over, and merged. That principle is transparency.

In this essential respect, we are still on course. A culture of decency has been preserved. Nothing, in that sense, has changed.

University

"Get a job with TBWA. You'll end up running an advertising agency."

Irritated by repeatedly losing senior staff to competitors, we published this full-page ad in Paris's *Le Figaro* daily newspaper in November 2006. Beneath the headline, we listed a dozen well-known figures from the business, all of whom were running agencies. Near the end of the page, there was a short explanation of how each of those people had learned his or her trade at TBWA. In other words, it was almost as if working at our French agency was a sure route to success in the advertising business. TBWA has always been considered, and always will be, an incubator for talent.

Success in a service industry such as ours is primarily a matter of people. I often tell those who run our offices around the world that they need to attract a disproportionate number of the talented people in their country. By disproportionate, I mean a larger share than the size of the office might warrant. The talent can come externally. But it can also be trained in-house. Too often, "training program" comes last on the management committee agenda. It's the item that gets postponed for lack of time. I always avoid postponing it, because in my opinion, training seems pretty crucial.

Personally speaking, I've always enjoyed teaching. At the end of the seventies, when TV advertising had been around for some thirty years in the US and some ten years in France, I was asked by the management of Young & Rubicam to conceive a training seminar on TV commercials. Finding a way of designing such an event for the people least likely to be receptive—creative talent—was a challenge. I worked on the project for more than a year with the help of our London office's creative director and the head of production at our office in New York. The result was quite convincing. The seminar was structured around five half-day modules: Idea and Execution, Power of Image, Meaning of Movement, Image and Sound, Single-mindedness…. We analyzed some two hundred commercials, the best available at the time. There were a few basic lessons on feature films for good measure. I was influenced by new wave director François Truffaut's book about Alfred Hitchcock and Joseph McBride's book on John Ford. Classic feature-film sequences were analyzed shot by shot, even second by second. Understanding how to storyboard a movie is critical if it's to be cut to a thirty-second spot. Among the exercises we devised, I remember the "telegram," or how to tell a story in less than twenty words. A film with an idea is easier to explain than a film without an idea.

So my first seminar was about TV. Thirty years later, I found myself designing a course for the School of Communication at Paris's prestigious Institute for Political Science. The chairman of that school asked me in 2006 to mentor a master's course. I set up a working group to determine the curriculum. Eighteen months later, we were up and running. In my welcome to the first year students, I explained the notion that communication is a discipline in its own right, with its own rules, its own talent, and its own history. The advertising industry deserves specific teaching courses. It cannot be dismissed as just another branch of marketing or social science. This was the basis upon which we had devised our masters. The fact that it was associated with the Institute for Political Science raised standards. It brought added cultural value, supplementary intelligence. "From rhetoric to digital science," was one professor's description of what we were setting out to teach.

Online Seminars

TBWA probably provides more teachers to this new school than any other firm. They illustrate their classes with cases selected from our emblematic campaigns. TBWA staff around the world know these campaigns by heart. An idea sold to an American insurance company can inspire a solution to a computer-programming company's problem in Thailand.... We've uploaded case studies, analyses, and speeches onto our intranet system. We've edited, classified, and arranged them by theme. The result is a kind of online university: a university of marketing and advertising, probably one of the most prolific in the business. We've called this UDMA—University of Disruption and Media Arts.

Our university contains sixty-two modules. Each is designed to serve a one-hour training session. Various sessions relate to our working practices, to Disruption and Media Arts, detailed case studies on international clients, specific lessons on subjects as varied as leadership and public speaking. About fifteen modules relate to digital expertise, new media approaches, and storytelling. One of the most popular is called "My First Disruption Day." It talks about how to organize the agenda for a Disruption Day and the pitfalls that need to be avoided, the fatal mistakes.

In a sense, what we have made is a virtual, interactive university. Every office can upload anything it likes onto it. Employees can use it to learn from their colleagues' experience. Training doesn't have to be hierarchical anymore. It ought to be horizontal. Peer-to-peer.

UDMA opens TBWA staff members' minds to the whole range of communications' disciplines. The world's increasing complexity and the exponential growth in subjects to be mastered would appear to make our goal of trying to be one step ahead on everything overly ambitious. Except that UDMA's true goal relates to what has always been said about education and culture. The more you learn, the more you become aware of how little you know. UDMA offers TBWA staff members a chance to discover where to find what they don't know.

256

Future Talent

Our training ideas don't stop there. Here's some more: Young Bloods, Tiger Academy, Very Short Very Cheap Film Festival.

John Hunt set up Young Bloods when he was head of our New York office. It's a program that offers several beginners an opportunity to conceive films and ads for our most important clients on their very first day in the office. This is not in any way an internship. We're treating beginners like experienced staff here. In 2003, John published a message to say that TBWA was going to be welcoming twelve of the best young creative people in the US. All any art-school student or advertising student had to do was send in an application. The only condition was that they must never have worked in an advertising agency before. We wanted fresh minds.

Thousands of people applied. HR short-listed the top one hundred. Our creative teams cut that short list to twenty. John Hunt selected the final twelve, not even knowing whether they were men or women. Intuitively, he "married" them in six pairs and off they went, working on important cases from the moment they started. One of the teams took part in a pitch that brought the New York office a major client, Nextel. The program turned out to be so fruitful that we exported the idea to Germany, to South Africa and China, to Japan and Malaysia and India and New Zealand. Since then, John Hunt has set up a world Young Blood community club. Young Bloods are now a part of our culture at TBWA. They bring fresh momentum and a big dose of enthusiasm into departments that need constant challenging. After a trial period of a year, if we're happy with them, we hire them permanently.

"Why try and hire superstars from outside the firm when we can find them and train them ourselves?" asks John Hunt. Most Young Bloods would probably have done as well in other agencies, but our program gives them a head start of a few years. Craig Allen, one of our first Young Bloods, left us three years ago. He has since designed the famous Old Spice "Smell Like a Man, Man" campaign, which won more prizes than any other in the US in 2011. More proof of the value of the Young Bloods program.

UDMA is for all those at TBWA. Young Bloods is for young creative talent. Tiger Academy is for future leaders. It brings the best people in the network together, about twenty of the most promising every year. It trains people to answer the question, "Why would anyone want me to be their boss?" One of the aims of the academy was to boost our most promising people's loyalty to TBWA. I don't feel we have been sufficiently successful in this. Our "retention factor" has not progressed. Joining the academy has not prevented some people from leaving. But those who do stay establish much stronger international bonds with their colleagues. They speak daily, or almost. They form a virtual community that strengthens our internal ties.

We have also set up a program that provides unfettered and playful opportunities by offering everyone a chance to direct. This is called the "Very Short Very Cheap Film Festival." Every single one of us—all twelve thousand TBWA staff—is offered the opportunity of shooting a thirty-second movie. At first, participants were encouraged to choose a brand we work for and make a film for it. Making films can cost next to nothing these days. In year one, John Hunt was sent several dozen movies. By year two, he was being sent several hundred. At that time, he decided that he would select the brand. Participants would be asked to work for a specific client. First Pedigree, the year after Absolut. Three hundred fifteen films from fifty different cities were made for Absolut. They were written and produced by creative talent, by Young Bloods, by account people and financial managers... Absolut ended up showing eight of them on YouTube. The agency recommended reshooting two clips with real budgets. These turned out to be "Absolut Hugs" from the Philippines and "Absolut Launderette" from Germany. Absolut broadcast these two commercials on major TV channels. The "Very Short Very Cheap Film Festival" had come of age.

UDMA, Young Bloods, Tiger Academy, Very Short Very Cheap Film Festival, and other similar programs... why bother? Why organize all these projects that take up so much money and time? Because they increase our chances of seeing tomorrow's talent at TBWA. We want our agency to top the list when the time comes for them to choose.

Half of the people who will be working at TBWA in ten years time have yet to join us. We should not forget that.

Vision

"Impossible is not a fact, it's an opinion."

These giant-sized words appeared on the outside of
the building. I was watching Muhammad Ali, thinking
he could have said them himself. It was raining. We
were in a gym. About one hundred people were
thronging around him. A few chairs had been set up
in an impromptu way. He sat down, soon joined by
members of his family, including his daughter Laila, a
super middleweight champ herself.

Images showing the famous Kinshasa fight against
George Foreman came into my mind. For eight rounds,
Ali had received blow after blow from a boxer much
more powerful than he was. He took direct hits to the
head without flinching, bunched up against the ropes.
His peerless legwork had been of no use to him. He
had not been able to whirl around his opponent the
way he usually did. He had lost his stylish presence.
That old haughty cool which had taken so many of
his opponents by surprise had left him. He hadn't
stood a chance. Then, what looked like powerlessness

261

turned out to be a tactic. An incredibly brave tactic. The plan was that, by allowing Foreman to punch Ali incessantly, Foreman would end up punching himself to exhaustion. By round eight, Foreman started to weaken. Muhammad Ali won the most brutal fight in his career. It was an improbable victory that proved what Adidas would be telling the world thirty years later: "Impossible is Nothing."

That spring day back in 2003, a few friends of Adidas had gathered in that gym. Dozens of kids were spinning around Ali. He would stroke their faces, shake any hands available, including ours. I was astonished to find that the legend was intact. Kids from the neighborhoods around Harlem, barely ten or twelve years old, were displaying incredible veneration. Ali was sick but sickness had failed to tarnish the charisma…. A few moments earlier, high up on a podium at a junction in the middle of Harlem, he had unveiled two giant posters. Each displayed a giant photograph. There was one of him, one of his daughter. The two portraits stood face-to-face, framing Adidas's new brand manifesto: "Impossible is just a big word thrown around by small men who find it easier to live in the world they've been given than to explore the power they have to change it. Impossible is not a fact. It's an opinion. Impossible is not a declaration. It's a dare. Impossible is potential. Impossible is temporary. Impossible is Nothing."

That night the film I've already mentioned was premiered on TV. Special-effects magic had allowed us to devise a fight between Ali and his daughter: a real-life fight. The legwork, the swerves, the blows. Everything was there. Down to Laila's uppercut to her Dad's chin and the admiring glance he gives her a few seconds later from his stool in the corner of the ring. His daughter's voice-over reminds us that everyone had advised Ali not to agree to that Kinshasa fight against Foreman, who would "destroy" him. He had done the impossible.

Adidas has always been authentic. The German brand is about everyone who plays sports, be they professional or amateur. It's not just about international stars. It actually enjoys being seen on dirt running tracks in the middle of housing projects. We needed to find one phrase to express everything Adidas believes in. Or rather, how Adidas knows what goes on inside every sportsman or sportswoman's mind as they compete. At whatever level. Amateur sports competitors and international stars have one thing in common: both see their most recent personal best as a wall ahead that is just too high to get over. Then they beat that previous record. The impossible ratchets up one notch further. Every time that happens, Sunday golfers, joggers, kids playing baseball, all know "Impossible is just an opinion."

Such was Adidas's vision at that time. Our job is about helping clients define the way they see their brands. Like many marketing words, "vision" seems clichéd. Still, we haven't found a better way of saying there's a future that hasn't happened yet, a future in the waiting. Vision is a mental image, an imaginary representation of how far a brand can reach.

We like to have that vision concentrated into a short phrase: "Think Different," "Impossible is Nothing," "Dogs Rule." A collection of two- or three-word phrases like that seems effortless. It's like they took only a few seconds to be found. They give that impression because they are just so right. To identify why they're good, you only need to think of all the possible alternatives. There were thousands of things to say about Apple, Adidas, or Pedigree. So why these slogans rather than any other? Because they capture the essence of a brand. They offer a starting point and an inspiration for a wide range of initiatives that will further define brand identity.

As soon as Adidas started saying, "Impossible is Nothing," an idea a day happened to make the phrase mean more. "Vertical Football" is one famous instance. On a giant poster, on top of a building in Tokyo, forty meters up, we painted a mini vertical soccer field. Two players hanging on cables played a game a few minutes long several times a day, flying through the air, repeatedly leaping acrobatically, kicking the ball on the volley. It was such a striking scene that three hundred TV channels across every continent relayed it. One idea in a Tokyo neighborhood was broadcast worldwide. CNN called it "Sky Soccer."

A soccer goalkeeper's body draws an arc as he dives. During soccer's World Cup in Germany, we built a bridge over the highway as you leave Munich airport: a bridge thirty-five feet high, following the curve of Oliver Kahn, Germany's national goalkeeper, as he went for the ball.... Two years later, we incorporated a picture of Chelsea goalkeeper Petr Cech into Vienna's big wheel, of Orson Welles fame. His arms proliferated into multiple Vishnu-like spokes, suggesting that no ball would ever get past him.

In New Zealand, our office looks after the All Blacks, the Rugby world champions. One day, they asked each of the players to give us a drop of their blood. Then they mixed it into the printer's ink used to make the posters. When these posters appeared in Auckland and Wellington, everyone knew they contained a bit of the players' blood. The poster was called: "Bonded by Blood." Imagine the impact in a country where All Black players are like gods.... When the All Blacks went to Europe for the World Cup in 2007, we filled glass capsules with a few grams of soil from rugby fields in New Zealand. When they got to Europe, the All Blacks scattered the samples of the earth of their homeland on European playing fields to infuse them with the spirit of their ancestors.... The list of such ideas, initiatives, and events is endless. They feed the brand's idea that "Impossible is Nothing." We call them "the ideas behind the idea."

Brand Manifestos

As soon as a brand's vision of itself has been identified, it means that the brand can adjust the things it does, from the specifications for new product development to packaging design to choosing new modes of distribution. Vision has to be behind all things. It has to take in everything. It serves as a yardstick.

A vision must be defined in a single phrase or just a handful of words. But it can also be helpful to develop a longer version, more detailed, more evocative. The term used for this is "brand manifesto." Here are two extracts from brand manifestos already mentioned above. The first relates to Standard Chartered Bank. The second to Apple. In the first case, we see the bank wanting to restore dignity to a business that is so often criticized by asking, "Can a bank balance its ambition with its conscience? As not everything in life that counts can be counted. Can it not only look at the profit it makes but how it makes that profit?" In the second instance, we have Apple celebrating creativity by declaring, "Here's to the crazy ones. The misfits. The rebels. The troublemakers. The round pegs in the square holes. The ones who see things differently. You can praise them, disagree with them, quote them, disbelieve them, glorify or vilify them. About the only thing you can't do is ignore them."

There is a Virgin Megastore on the Champs-Elysées Avenue in Paris that is housed in an especially theatrical building. When it was opened, some people called it "a cathedral of music." Which is why when Chief Executive Patrick Zelnick asked us to look after the launch, we thought we'd go beyond the usual retailer campaign discourse boasting of the wide range of products and the attractiveness of their low pricing. We considered that the Megastore was the temple to the music industry. So we announced, "There can never be too much space for music…" The words that accompanied this slogan sound like a manifesto: "Turn up the volume. Music is for making your eyes water, your hair stand on end, to get crowds on their feet. We're for music that brings silence, emotional silence. We want to be children of the most powerful force on earth. Music."

Apple celebrates creativity. Virgin pays tribute to music. Both brands have given themselves a role to play. I must have employed that expression hundreds of time when telling clients about their brands. As early as 1980, we fell into a habit of saying, "A brand should never be satisfied with its rank. It has to give itself a role to play."

Here's another example. Pedigree. Paul Michaels, Mars's chief executive, signed a manifesto about a new vision for the brand that was printed into a little yellow book amusingly entitled "Dogma." In it, he says Pedigree cannot just be a leader in the dog-food sector. It has to aim higher. It has to be the brand that makes you love dogs. "From a dog-food company to a dog-lover's company" is the way we put it. Overnight, Pedigree reps started calling on buyers at Walmart or Carrefour bringing their dogs with them. Product managers who didn't like dogs were transferred to other divisions in Mars. The corporation launched a large-scale operation to encourage adopting abandoned dogs…. A tidal wave of sincerity broke over the Pedigree brand.

When I reread our manifestos, I am reminded of how important it is to add meaning to the brands with which we are entrusted. Manifestos offer concrete vision. They communicate brand vision in everyday language. Adidas, Pedigree, and Apple, each in its way, have chosen to aim higher. Much higher.

Companies On the Go

In the early eighties, Pepsi's boss was the charismatic John Sculley. The firm was nipping at Coca-Cola's heels. Commercials starring Michael Jackson or Lionel Richie were all over TV. The press was full of praise. At that time, Steve Jobs was still under thirty. He wanted a CEO for Apple. Someone who could stand by him to consolidate the success of the corporation he had founded. In those days, Apple was not yet a mass-market company. Steve met with Sculley, not to interview him but to ask him just one question. That question has become world-famous: "Do you want to sell sugar water for the rest of your life, or do you want to come with me and change the world?" Sculley's success at Pepsi was such that his future was brilliant and safe. Financial ease, power over tens of thousands of employees, peer recognition…. None of that meant anything compared to the challenge Steve Jobs was offering: "Change the world." John Sculley joined Steve Jobs.

Apple changes our lives every day. It has done us a fantastically good deed by making computers accessible to all. You may feel Apple is a case apart. That sport shoes and dog food cannot afford to be as ambitious. I don't believe that. Every corporation has to give itself the job of changing the world. Even in a tiny way. Otherwise, business is pure cynicism. The thousands of dogs that have been adopted thanks to Pedigree and the kids who play on Adidas-sponsored basketball courts offer living proof. There's no such thing as a minor contribution.

Vision is about giving yourself a trajectory. Without vision, the meaning of how a brand affects everyday life can get lost. Vision gives employees a sense that they belong to a company on the move, with all the entrepreneurial values that implies. Vision is commitment. It inspires action and sorts it. It is a precondition for things to happen.

Today, brands are judged as much by the initiatives they take as by the products they sell. I have already mentioned Best Buy, which is known for its sales excellence, which rests on a brand vision that can be summarized as "Serving, Not Selling." For instance, Best Buy encourages customers to tweet its salespeople for advice right through the day. This is good after-sales. Best Buy doesn't stop there. It wants even people who have never set foot in one of its stores to tweet staff. In other words, Best Buy employees spend almost as much time talking to people they've never met as selling stuff to actual in-store customers.

In France, at least three of our clients are exemplary in terms of the number of initiatives they launch: SNCF French Railways, Super U, and McDonald's. Let's start with SNCF French Railways, France's state-owned railroad corporation. Its boss, Guillaume Pepy, is constantly imagining new programs to make this company the European leader in its sector. Passengers complain they don't get enough information? An app called SNCF Direct allows passengers detailed real-time information. Four million people downloaded this app within months. Paper railway tickets seem out of date? These days you just show the ticket inspector your iPhone. A bar code containing everything they need to know acts as an e-ticket. No more waiting in line, no more ticket machines, no more punching in. Gradually, this state-owned corporation is introducing into its stations daycare centers, repair shops, medical labs, dry-cleaners, supermarkets, and fast-food outlets. All these ideas are designed to relieve travelers who are strapped for time. French Railways works for the senior traveler, too. They'll deliver your bags to your home, making travel a pleasure again for many older people.... The economic climate may be tough, but SNCF is getting to know its customers better and serving them better, day by day. It is determined to do this, it is a public utility evolving into a service company.

Super U is the fastest-growing food retailer in France. It does more than just keep prices low by putting the squeeze on suppliers. Under the aegis of Serge Papin, its president, it is constantly finding ways to innovate. It has decided that the majority of its food products must be grown less than thirty miles from point of sale. It supports more than one thousand organic milk producers in France. It is protecting local employment by choosing locally grown, regional, and seasonal produce first. It is refusing to sell endangered fish species. It is cutting out waste, notably in packaging. It is a standard-bearer for a sustainable agriculture that combines productivity and food safety. Finally, in a major step, it has undertaken to voluntarily ban some still-permitted substances in its products, where there is any doubt as to their safety. In other words, long ahead of any legislative constraints, it is anticipating customers' legitimate health concerns in deciding what goes on the shelves. Major retailers like Super U no longer just mechanically distribute the goods they sell, and they no longer lag behind the big brand names that fill their shelves. In many crucial respects, socially and otherwise, they are actually ahead of them. Super U's campaign says U stores are for the good of everyone, meaning producers, intermediaries, consumers, and citizens.

The last example is McDonald's. Over the last ten years McDonald's France, under the leadership of Jean-Pierre Petit, has launched a wide range of initiatives. It has signed a farmers' charter. It has introduced innovative youth-employment policies. It guarantees responsible product sourcing. It has entered into partnership with the French Ministry of Education and with academics. It has set up a waste-product disposal plan together with the French Association of Mayors. Its restaurants will only use renewable energy.... McDonald's used to be regarded as emblematic of US capitalism (not something the French press is particularly well disposed toward). For this reason, in the past, the company had a tendency to act in an introvert way. It advertised its products, not itself. It hid behind the product. One day, it decided to speak out, through a series of firm commitments. The list of McDonald's France's civic initiatives is endless.

Quest for Meaning

The word "purpose" is occurring with increasing frequency in the mouths of corporate managers. They talk about "brand purpose" or "company purpose." At a time when the world economy seems disorientated; when, following financial deregulation, there is an unsettling sense of disorder; when people in the old democracies and in emerging nations are worried about the future; it is interesting to note how this word has returned to favor in business circles. A "purpose" is not just a goal. It implies determination. It implies a quest for meaning.

Marc Pritchard, global marketing and brand-building officer at Procter & Gamble, and one of the most influential voices in our profession, made a speech to the Association of National Advertisers in October 2010 about the notion of "purpose." Here are a few extracts from this speech, which earned a great deal of US press comment: "People are no longer spectators to the intractable social and environmental problems of the world. They're stepping up and they're taking actions. And they expect us to do the same. And this changing world means that people want to know what's besides our brands and what's besides our company. They want to know if we share their values. Therefore interested in making a difference in the world and in their lives and not just in making money." And also this: "I believe that means we need to shift and move out of the selling products business and move into the business of improving life." Marc Pritchard concludes: "It means shifting from marketing to serving."

Naturally, such assertions provoke a degree of skepticism. Especially in Europe. We believe that business needs to mind its own…business. Pronouncements such as Marc Pritchard's sound like an attempt at making multinational corporations more acceptable. I can testify, however, that this speech was made in a spirit of total sincerity. I can testify to the degree to which Procter & Gamble brands' plans were modified to take account of this new vision. Each of those brands was given a sense of purpose over and above its product benefit. Thus, Procter & Gamble managers explain that Pampers has switched from "a benefit of superior dryness" to "an ideal of baby development."

Firms of Endearment is a book whose authors analyze the performance of thirty corporations who, they say, are governed by a purpose. Among others, these include Google, Best Buy, Whole Foods, Southwest Airlines, and Johnson & Johnson. They note that such companies never establish shareholder interests as a primary goal. Employees, customers, suppliers, and consumers all get priority. They also note that these corporations are considerably more profitable than others. That was a major revelation to me. If a corporation's purpose is not just making money, then it will actually end up making more money than expected. Employee turnover is lower, productivity is higher, margins are more resilient, and so share price is healthier.

Jim Stengel used to sit in Marc Pritchard's chair at Procter & Gamble. This is what he told Roy Spence of GSD&M about Pampers: "We asked ourselves what's the one thing that every mother cares about? And what she cares about is her baby's development in every way. So we began to seize that idea. And we switched from being a brand about functional benefit to a brand that helps mothers around the world with their baby's physical, social, and emotional development. It started to get people inspired. It got the imagination going. The agenda for innovation started to change.... We identified "sound sleep" as a key to healthy development. We began asking questions like what can Pampers' role be in helping babies have deep, healthy sleep so they can wake up with energy, with rejuvenation and better brain development? We did clinical studies in that area."

We've come a long way.... When I started out in this business, I would never have thought that a corporation that sold detergents and diapers would do such things. I would never have imagined I'd be conducting Disruption Days discussing five-year or ten-year visions with my clients. I could never have suspected that our business would be about designing iPhone apps, chatting on social networks, or creating events relayed by news reporters around the world. I would never have imagined that the best is to come. That everything, or nearly, is yet to be invented.

The great French poet Paul Valery once charmingly wondered, "What would become of us if we could not count on the help of things that do not exist?"

Wells

"If we were modest, we would be perfect."

This provocative statement was made by Dick Rich, Mary Wells's partner, two years after the launch of their agency, Wells Rich Greene.

Mary Wells and her partners embodied the best of American advertising in its golden era. The agency they founded in 1966 experienced the fastest internal growth in history, winning many prestigious clients such as Benson & Hedges, Cadbury Schweppes, American Motors, and Procter & Gamble. It also designed some of the most influential campaigns in the business. The campaign that made Mary Wells famous revived a failing airline, Braniff. Mary had all the planes painted bright colors. She got Gucci to design a new uniform for the hostesses. It was, as the slogan said, "The end of the plain plane."

A play on words invited Americans to take a break and smoke a Benson & Hedges cigarette, making the most of their unusual length. One ad showed a stylish

275

gentleman's Benson & Hedges cigarette sliced in two by elevator doors. (In those days, people smoked in elevators!) Many other commercials of that sort were to follow. No one in advertising had ever dared damage a product in a campaign before. From that time on, the brand's stiff and formal British image was never the same again. Overnight, Bensons became cool or, as people used to say back then, "hip." Wells was also the agency that came up with the super-famous poster designed by Milton Glaser that has been copied millions times since: the one that says, "I Love New York," with a red heart instead of the word "love."

Mary Wells was known to ask her creative teams to work for clients she didn't yet have. Then she'd fix up a meeting with the chief executive of the company in question and expose him to slogans her writers had come up with. On one such occasion, she met the CEO of Braniff and married him. This was one of the first "long-distance" marriages, as the expression goes. Her husband, Harding Lawrence, lived in Dallas while she was in New York. All the gossip magazines were wild about this ostentatious couple. A few years later, Mary Wells resigned the Braniff contract to take on the TWA account. Then she switched to PanAm, a prestigious airline no longer with us, though the memory of its famous Park Avenue building that slices Park Avenue in two lives on.

Madison Avenue

Mary Wells of Wells Rich Greene was the first woman to make the cover of *Fortune* magazine. No woman before her had ever chaired a company listed on the Stock Exchange. "Feminism was still so new, it was just a rumor on the East and West coasts," she told the *New York Times*. She listed her agency in 1968. Then decided to de-list in 1974 after losing a few clients. This shuttling in and out allowed her to buy back her agency at a markedly lower price. Her own wealth increased visibly.

Buckets of money poured through the advertising business in the years that followed the so-called creative revolution. The previous generation, epitomized by David Ogilvy, was swept aside. "The lunatics have taken over the asylum," was his response. One of the most prominent figures in the business in those years was Jerry Della Femina. He acted as a consultant to the screenwriters of *Mad Men*, which is partially based on a book of memoirs he published at the age of thirty-four in 1970. I have often eaten lunch at his restaurant on Manhattan's Fifty-Fourth Street. Now he's opened a new agency, probably his fourth. "Once a Mad Man, always a Mad Man," is how he put it to the *New York Times*.

Mary Wells was the Queen of Madison Avenue. In 1990, a few days before a New York press conference was called to tell the world she'd sold us her company, Jean-Claude Boulet and I spent a weekend as her guest on Mustique in the West Indies. Mary Wells lived like a

277

Hollywood movie star, she lived like the Great Gatsby. I've seen her estates. I've counted the number of her servants. I counted the number of private jets that crossed the Atlantic for her daughter's wedding. Most of these belonged to clients or former clients such as Estée Lauder. Mary Wells asked David Niven to add to her copywriters' excellent scripts the patrician gravitas of his voice. In this way, they recorded a few voice-overs together. They made friends. He introduced her to many stars, from Frank Sinatra to Grace Kelly, who was not above chatting with the wives of clients Mary asked to stay at Cap Ferrat, on the French Riviera, where she had a house. Sometimes, Giovanni Agnelli, the chief executive and principal shareholder of Fiat, the respected Italian carmaker, would water-ski over from Monte Carlo across the bay.

In 1969, the financial press told the world she was the best-paid businessperson in America. In any case, her income was way above other advertising executives, all of whom were male. One famous New York opinion-maker once described Mary Well's life of luxury as, "Wonderful beyond wonderful." *Ad Age* said, "She is advertising's most widely publicized symbol of glamour, success, wealth, brains and beauty." The words that come up most regularly in the interviews she gave were "adrenalin," "energy," "non-conformism," "irreverent," "theatrical," "magnificent." After she sold us her business, she solemnly declared, "The Queen is dead."

In 2002, she published a memoir entitled *A Big Life in Advertising*. A reporter from the *New York Times* interviewed me when it came out. With respect and without acrimony, wanting to state the facts, I explained that Wells Rich Greene would forever remain one of the most creative advertising agencies the world had ever known. But I added that Mary had taken a back seat for too long. When we arrived, we found the business in nowhere near the same condition.

This was not overly harsh. But Mary didn't appreciate it.

Insights

One day, a reporter asked her about British advertising. This was in the seventies. London agencies were firing on all cylinders. Beginners, such as me, felt that the creative revolution had crossed the Atlantic and that London had supplanted New York. Mary Wells did not agree. This is what she had to say about the supposed supremacy of British advertising: "This is an opinion frequently expressed in British circles. And it is true that British advertising is often witty and sometimes funny. But Americans know how to explore emotions such as hunger, sex, fatherhood and so on. I believe that we are still ten years ahead." She was right. British advertising kept and still keeps that British reserve. Whereas American advertising at its best is better than any other at grabbing the desires and emotions of the people it addresses. It knows how to touch people.

There is a good word to describe sharp perceptions in our everyday lives. The word is "insights." One American ad asks, "Have you reached that difficult stage when your boss is younger than you are?" That's a good instance of insight. As it happens, there is no equivalent word in my own language. Insight rests on identifying some small detail, the relevance and accuracy of which seems instantly obvious the minute it is expressed. Insights are incursions into people's lives and minds. They steal in and grab something hidden. Any ad that captures an insight greatly increases its impact.

Mary Wells had a powerful sense of observation. One ad was enough to turn an underrated pill into an indispensable aid to people who love life. I mean Alka-Seltzer. A man sits at the edge of his bed, clutching his head in his hands. His wife has her back to him. Over and over again, he murmurs, "I can't believe I ate the whole thing, I can't believe I ate the whole thing." Quality of acting and a plain setting make this a classic among ads. It propelled Alka-Seltzer into a new league. What had been just another medicine became an accomplice to living the good life. Indeed Mary ended her Alka-Seltzer ads with a slogan that said, "You're nobody if you don't take Alka-Seltzer." She also brought about a leap in sales by recommending that the packets should be sold in twos, with the obvious implication that two packets worked better than one. Within a few years, sales had exploded. Today, fifty years later, most people who use Alka-Seltzer still follow her advice.

"Women no longer want to look young at any price, they know every age has its own beauty"; "A baby that sleeps well at night has a better chance of increasing

280

physical and mental capacity by day." These are two insights that inspired not just advertising campaigns but also initiatives and new products from Olay and Pampers. Johnson & Johnson launched a corporate campaign called "Having a baby changes everything." It's hard to find parents who disagree. P&G has its own way of defining an insight: "It is a discovery about the consumer that elicits an emotional reaction along the lines of 'you obviously understand me.'"

At TBWA, we had the opportunity to really get to understand what turns video-game players on. These people often spend a very large part of their lives indulging their favorite occupation. You might say— here's the insight—that they only really feel alive when they sit at their consoles. This observation inspired a film we wrote for Sony PlayStation in Britain a few years back. It showed a series of odd characters reciting strangely poetic, though stiff language. One by one, a succession of them describes what they do: "In the day, I do my job, I ride the bus."; "But at night I live a life of exhilaration."; "I have engaged in violence, even indulged in it..."; "I've exhibited disregard for life, limb and property..."; "I have commanded armies and conquered worlds..."; The last person to speak concludes, "For though I've lived a double life, at least I can say: I have lived..." And it is true that Sony PlayStation lets people live a double life.

To identify insights, you have to be curious. You have to be observant. Sometimes, observation can lead to recommendations that go beyond advertising or even beyond business. In his book, John Hunt mentions one

281

poignant example of an insight. In many African countries, well water is carried miles. Often, this is a job for children. They walk long distances every day to make sure their families have water. Those same kids love merry-go-rounds even if, in the absence of power, they have to hand-crank them. Now, many villages use a merry-go-round to drive a water pump, preferably near a school. And the pump sends the water to their homes. The kids no longer need to walk miles to carry their buckets. Fetching water can be fun. John uses this story to show that insights seem obvious when expressed in words. But they don't come into one's mind easily. As John puts it, "Our job is to turn facts into insights."

In the French edition of this book, I left a number of English words or phrases untranslated. I use words like "insight," "sense of purpose," "single-mindedness" because they are hard to translate accurately. Many of my fellow Frenchmen dislike this. They want the language pure. But there are some words which, when they are translated, lose a part of their meaning. The fact that a word may be hard to translate from one language to another says something. It shows that the word expresses a concept unknown to the destination language, or at least so unfamiliar to it that no term has been devised. Rather than go for an approximation, it seems better to leave the English term intact. So I shall continue to encourage French people to use words like "insight" that enrich our conceptual tool kit. If French advertising professionals stopped using those words, they would put themselves at a disadvantage to American and British competitors by depriving themselves of fertile avenues of thought.

They might also prove Mary Wells right. The science of insight would remain an American specialty.

X Generation

"What scares you most?"

"What's your favorite time of day? What makes you angry?" Three hundred people from sixteen different countries were answering this list of unusual and sometimes intimate questions. A far cry from the typical research questionnaire. We were trying to get inside the heads of Generation Y, the people also known as "millennials." A multitude of responses from around the world was going to be collated into a collective portrait.

Yann-Arthus Bertrand is a French photographer and film director who is known for his environmental activism. In 2009, he organized an amazing traveling exhibit, first launched at Paris's prestigious Grand Palais. This was called "Six Billion Others." His team also interviewed people from around the planet. Their aim was to build a collective image of who we are. They weren't interested in aggregates, in anonymously synthesized data, but in meaningful and sensitive accounts gathered over a limited time. Their goal was to reflect what we all have in common. An Afghan fisherman, a Vietnamese tailor, a Danish sculptor, a Brazilian farmer, a Buddhist monk, a Parisian bistro-owner discuss their dreams, their fears, their aims, their hopes. Then, early in 2009, the Grand Palais was filled with Mongolian yurt tents. Each tent housed a filmed interview projected on screen, three hundred interviews in all, chosen from thousands. All of them poignant portraits of our contemporaries. Flipping through the show's Visitor Book, it is striking to see how many visitors said they found the show moving. They were "happy to be counted among the six billion inhabitants of our planet."

Yann-Arthus Bertrand's purpose was to provide a portrait of the world's diversity. It was this adventure that inspired us to invest in having a better understanding of the largest generation there has ever been on earth, Generation Y. A Google search delivers some three million references about how these people behave. You would have thought everything to say about the millennials had been said. Except you can always go further by trying to get under people's skin, into their hearts and their heads. By trying to feel what they actually feel. Our questionnaire was designed to encourage interviewees to reveal intimate thoughts. We adopted Yann-Arthus Bertrand's cinematographic style, shooting people close-up in portrait format, facing the camera.

Depicting Millennials

We started out one Saturday morning in New York City. Thirty millennials from around the city showed up. Emmanuel André, network COO, supervised the event. He found people on the street who seemed to have that special something, that distinctive magnetic quality. He asked if they wanted to participate in an artistic project. Emmanuel did not admit to being in advertising. He just said, "Give me one hour of your time," brought them into a studio, and asked, "What's the most important thing that ever happened to you?" "If you ruled the world, what would be the first thing you'd do?" And so on. There were twelve questions.

Emmanuel realized that he had collected much more than just thoughts or ideas. He had succeeded in capturing intimacy. He noticed that little things like gestures, expressions, hesitations, uncertainty, body language all tell us as much as the answers themselves. The experience was repeated in sixteen other cities around the world. Three hundred thirty-seven conversations were recorded. The answers were edited regardless of geography. If you wander through the photographs and film clips recorded on an interactive platform, what you discover is the voice of a generation. Planners in our offices use this as raw material in their recommendations to clients. Some of these would like to extend the study to see how the young interviewees feel about their brands. They want a genuine reflection, they want authentic reactions. They are no longer satisfied with disembodied quantitative data.

We should take a look at Generation X in the same way. Generation X comprises people born between 1960 and 1980. Robert Capa called them "Generation X" because he found their identity hard to pin down. They moved through an era without a squeak. They were treated like royalty by their parents, who were often divorced. Generation X remained in their parents' shadow. In truth, the big behavioral divide does not come between Generation X and Generation Y, but between these two generations and the baby-boomers who preceded them.

Generation X and Generation Y have many things in common. Their standard of living has not progressed beyond their parents'. They are called young till they are past thirty. They face unemployment. They want to live life to the fullest, but they no longer trust work to help them achieve that goal. They do not know the meaning of the word "career." They are keenly and anxiously aware that we are asking the planet for more than it can give us.

Postmodern Generations

Generation X has had to adapt to the Internet. Generation Y was born to it. As is well known, its members are called "digital natives." More surprisingly perhaps, Gen Xers now also spend more time on the Net than watching TV. They spend as much time social-networking as does Generation Y. The behavior pattern of the two generations is converging. What we are dealing with here are the two first "postmodern" generations.

These generations are not hostile to brands. But they know all about the mechanics of marketing; they can spot a trick. We must respect this in the way we work. Above all, they don't go crazy about the same brands as their predecessors. They love Apple, Nike apparently less so. Many brands are in for a surprise, especially as young Internet users see themselves as web experts capable of influencing others. Large numbers of them discuss the advantages and disadvantages of products in forums. Many post brand logos on their Facebook profiles. Brands are a part of their personal identity.

They are not hostile to advertising, either. According to a study organized by Microsoft, 24 percent have downloaded advertisements on YouTube or social network sites, compared with 30 percent who download music videos. That isn't a big gap. I believe that they will go on sharing and promoting the best ads. The growth of online video will generate new forms of creativity. This trend is already visible on iAd, Apple's ad platform. When it was launched, Steve Jobs criticized the poor quality of most Internet advertising and showed how iAd would enable new forms of advertising to blossom. He launched the program by showing an ad from Nissan, another of our clients, for their electric car. He pleaded for new forms of creativity in online advertising.

Every year, we make dozens of films that reflect the oddball humor of the current generations. These films are willfully off-the-wall, willfully nonsensical, and often obscure. For instance, there is a famous commercial in which a grandfather transforms everything he touches into Skittles. He cannot lift his grandson into his arms, otherwise…. Another brand of candy has a Japanese person teaching his son the bagpipes…. Every day, creative talent in New York and London from Generation X and Generation Y dreams up scripts people of my generation don't always get. But young people on the Internet find these films hilarious. They love reenacting them with their friends. Amateur videos spread like wildfire. There are dozens of versions around. Viewers vote on them. Suddenly, there you are voted best director of such-and-such a movie's remake.

Humor divides generations. Music brings them together. I've met people from all three generations at Adele, FM Laeti, or Patti Smith concerts. My love of music dates back to the days when, from the northern coasts of France, we could pick up Radio Caroline, the British pirate station, which inspired the movie *Pirate Radio*. Somehow, the world seemed a bigger place. Music accompanied, or rather preceded, that process. The increasing sophistication of the Beatles' arrangements, Jimi Hendrix's torrential solos, the theatrical craziness of the Who, Pink Floyd's frantic psychedelics all gave us the sense we were living through a powerful crescendo. My sharpest memories of the decade have to do with a feeling of progress, a feeling that music was gradually opening out and blossoming. I still regard each changing year of the sixties as a new threshold, a new stage in the forward march of music. François Bégaudeau captured the essence of that sensation better than anyone in a book about Mick Jagger. He says, "The decade just kept steadily rising higher and higher." He speaks of the "upward curve of the temperature in the cauldron of the sixties." He adds that this decade was the most "transforming of the century." Musicians formed the links in a universal chain. Countless musical currents blended together. Groups bounced off each other, boosting their collective energies. This energy just kept on swelling from recording to recording, from concert to concert. Bégaudeau captures the spirit of a generation, its beat, in a musical sense. When I read his book, I supposed that we belonged to the same generation. We felt the same forward motion, our hearts pounded to the same vibe. I was very surprised to discover that he was only thirty-four years old when he wrote the book. He is a schoolteacher. He also writes for the most famous of all French movie magazines, *Les Cahiers du Cinéma*. He played his own part in *Entre les murs*, which won the Palme d'Or at the Cannes Film Festival in 2008. He was born in 1971. He is part of Generation X.

In other words, music has built bridges between generations. For the first time in recent history, parents and kids are both wild about the same hits, old and new. My twenty-year-old son and I have watched *8 Mile*, the Eminem movie, together. He knows the early hits of Liverpool's Merseybeat scene as well as I do. I experienced the evolution of rock into pop into punk and new wave and house and techno from a distance. Our kids have experienced each of those steps at close range. Every generation is defined by the music it listens to, but these days younger generations are no longer so exclusive. They do not reject the earlier stages. They add and accumulate them.

For Pepsi, we made a film that shows Bob Dylan passing the torch to Will.I.am. Bob Dylan performs "Forever Young" on stage. Will.I.am takes over, morphing the words so they fit into a hip-hop beat. A voice-over sums it up: "Every generation refreshes the world."

You Say You Want a Revolution

I belong to a generation that believed it was going to change the world. A generation that created the Free Speech Movement in Berkeley and many other movements around the world. In France we had the May 1968 riots. Our dreams never materialized. They were just student fantasies. The world we built is a lot more dangerous and a lot less based on solidarity than the world we aspired to then.

My generation is also the generation that saw the rise of advertising. It must carry its fair share of the criticism for the birth of a society where superfluous goods have become presented as vital necessities. We took comfort in the fact that the economic growth we were feeding would allow for a redistribution of income. In the end, we only saw the good side about what we were doing. The fact is that, in its own small way, our industry has also contributed to the injustices and imbalances of our age.

The torch is passing from our generation to one that is at least partially disillusioned and disenchanted. A political philosopher speaks of a "painful historical moment." He emphasizes that this is not the end of history, but a historical dead-end. He also says that the generations to come will bear an extraordinary responsibility. They will have to redress the course of history. Imperceptibly, they are doing just that. They are taking part in an invisible revolution. Little by little they are accomplishing everything my generation talked about without ever succeeding in doing it.

First and foremost, they want to make the world a more socially aware place. Environmentally and socially responsible initiatives are becoming the new norm. Industry will reduce pollution. Business will become more and more transparent. Gradually, income differentials will diminish. Solidarity will become a watchword. My generation said it wanted to see a more helpful world. The generations to come will make it happen. Never will our individual destinies come to depend so much on our collective destiny.

Next point: the generation to come will be "flat," and will make the world work horizontally. Networking and communication are undermining hierarchical or vertical management. People have less respect for authority. Authority at work will be based exclusively on competence. This trend is visible now in the way big corporations in my homeland make senior appointments. Expertise is the most sought-after quality. That has not always been so. In the future, hierarchies will subside. A.G. Lafley, Procter & Gamble's former head, remodeled the company entirely by ensuring that decisions were no longer to be taken as high up as possible, but lower down, where people know the issues best.

Finally, the generation to come will make the world more "local." We all live in fear of a globalized homogenized culture. One that is uniform. One that is simplistic. This apprehension is only partly justified. The Internet has not stifled local cultures. It has given them somewhere to be, to grow strong and expand from. We are rediscovering forgotten traditions, languages nearing extinction, rare craftsmanship, outlandish literatures, exotic customs. The beauty of the Internet also lies in its capacity to allow us all to make new encounters on a very local level.

The spirit of the late sixties may not have changed the world, but it created a lasting sense of community. Twenty years later, that spirit has fueled the development of the Internet. Maybe the Internet is the closest connection between my generation and the generations that have come since. Monique Dagnaud, a well-known scientist in my country, wrote an article with a catchy title. It's called "Worldwide Web, a Laboratory Experiment in Friendly Capitalism." She says that the Internet's collective imagination is full of the cultural after-effects of the sixties. The values of the era—disinterestedness, the universal sharing of knowledge—are vital to the Internet today. Internet users may not know it, but they have remained faithful to the spirit of those times.

January 28, 2011. Wael Ghonim was arrested on Tahrir Square, in Cairo, Egypt. He was the first Egyptian to call for a demonstration against Hosni Mubarak's regime. Thanks to Facebook, thousands of his fellow citizens heard his appeal. So did the police. When he was released from jail twelve days later, we were told that he was just thirty years of age. His job: marketing director for Egypt and the Middle East at Google.

A regional manager at the Internet's number-one company launched a revolution that could not have happened without the Internet. The episode is emblematic. It symbolizes a generation.

Yogurt

"We've been on the wrong track for as near as twenty years," said Pierre Dupasquier when we were talking one day.

He was chief executive of Danone, now world leader in dairy products, and the holding company that owns Dannon USA. At that time, Danone was still just a division in a group called BSN, the other parts of which were Evian (water), Lu (cookies) and Kronenbourg (beer). This was in 1983. I had been working for Danone for more than ten years. There were campaigns for yogurt—plain, flavored, with added fruit, with added vitamins—and campaigns for creamy desserts. All in all, Danone was sending out a wide range of messages. None spoke of the health benefits of Danone products. Danone's main purpose, its raison d'etre, as the French say, had become lost along the way.

Danone was set up in 1919 in Spain by a man named Isaac Carasso. He had taken his son's nickname as a brand name. Danone was short for Daniel, a Spanish

297

version of Danny. Before the Second World War, Daniel Carasso brought Danone to France. Like his father, he first sold through pharmacies.

Decades went by. The brand's original culture became diluted. Danone became a mainstream dairy desserts manufacturer. They sold "pleasure" food in supermarkets, an approach that was far removed from the original "food for health" posture. The reason why can be found in the context of the era. Marketing was in its infancy. All kinds of initiatives were taking place, without much thought being given to coherence…. Pierre Dupasquier was alarmed by what he observed. But at the same time, he was in profound disagreement over the group's international strategy with Antoine Riboud, BSN's historic boss. Riboud had propelled BSN to number-one status in the French food industry. He continued to buy every single major independent French brand he could find. Some of these acquisitions, such as a couple of Dijon mustard brands or, even further from the corporation's core business, Pommery and Lanson champagnes, just seemed too nonstrategic to Pierre. He was thinking in global terms. His boss was visionary in his own way, but he was having trouble thinking outside France. Yet if Danone was to survive competition from world giants like Unilever, General Mills, General Foods, or Kraft, it was going to need to strengthen its international position.

Pierre Dupasquier has the intelligence to express ideas as plainly as possible. As far as he was concerned, this was a matter of common sense. The question he was asking was, "What are the product categories in which we have strong positions and where there are no real global leaders?" The answer was obvious: yogurts with Danone and mineral water with Evian. What was needed was massive investment into those two brands at a global level. Funding such investment would mean getting rid of everything else. It would mean selling champagne brands like Pommery, Lanson, and many other brands as well. Fifteen years later, this is exactly what Antoine Riboud's son Franck did. His reconfiguring of Danone has been a huge success.

Disagreement between Pierre Dupasquier and Antoine Riboud hardened to an unmanageable extent. At the end of 1983, Pierre left Danone. He went to the US to become CEO of Johnson & Johnson. He has had a brilliant second half of his career. His legacy at Danone has been a belated recognition and revival of the company's roots in health. Personally, I have been no more than a messenger between him and his successors. Many outside consultants have tried to claim credit for initiating the company's strategic transformation into a health-product company. The truth is that Danone owes this to its former boss, Pierre Dupasquier.

Institute for Health

A few years later, the president of Dannon USA came home to France from the US to take over Danone France. He advised me to look at what Kellogg's had been doing recently. I sent a strategic planner across the Atlantic, who returned bearing an impressive report detailing all the programs that Kellogg's was managing in the health field. These were impressive by force of numbers, but they were also scattered and lacking a backbone.

We recommended to Danone that they set up a Danone Institute of Health. The idea was to fund a place where the company's researchers might cross paths with other doctors, nutritionists, and scientists. The aim would be to conduct in-depth studies into the connection between eating and health. I took part in some of the early meetings with the doctor in charge of the institute. His interest was in pure research. Mine was in applied research. I was focusing on grasping how research might generate new product development. I may have been premature in assessing future benefits in advertising terms, but many promising new avenues were explored. They related to life expectancy, immune systems, infant feeding.... Whenever we came across research results that seemed like they might interest people, we produced films to explain them to the general public.

The campaign's theme was "Entreprendre pour la Santé," which means "Take Action for Health." *Entreprendre* is a French verb related to the word "enterprise" that does not exist in English. It is a beautiful word particularly when associated with our most precious asset, health.

Danone was making no claims here. There were no extravagant promises. No overselling. The company merely indicated the path it had chosen. The slogan and the campaign were strikingly relevant. Danone was entering into a higher sphere, but with no arrogance. We produced a dozen films. Each was structured in the same way, with a voice-over halfway through, saying: "Tomorrow, thanks to research, our diet will become our first line of defense." This belief is inspired by the two-thousand-year-old writings of Hippocrates. One of these commercials touched on life expectancy. It showed a young child looking not like his grandfather, but like his great-grandfather. Another one on infant food took place in a kindergarten. Another film about longevity was set in a retirement home.

The Danone Institute's campaign ran for many years. The heads of every packaged goods company who visited our agency during those years were highly envious of the program. They often asked us to devise something similar for their brands, a campaign in the same vein. We rarely succeeded.

In 1994, Antoine Riboud decided to switch the name of the company he had built from BSN to Danone. He illustrated his reasoning by describing "a Texan cab-driver who, like every good American" had built up a portfolio of stocks. He supposed that such a person might want to invest in a European food business. He might choose Nestlé because he knew their products, whereas BSN meant nothing to him. That is why Antoine Riboud chose Danone as the new name for his company. Danone was only one division. But it was the division that meant the most. The day he told the financial press about the change, he made a speech that revolved around the brand's legacy of health products and quoted the institute as an initiative that had been one of the most telling indicators of where Danone's future lay.

That was twenty years ago. Competition from supermarket private labels has meant that only the brands with the strongest values have survived. Since it started "taking action for health," Danone has strengthened its position everywhere in the world. Danone has become market leader in nearly all the countries where it operates, with a strong advantage over the runner-up. Bernard Hours, Danone's managing director, recently gave an interview to French business school HEC's internal journal. He said, "Danone's job is to make most people healthy by healthy eating. This isn't just business strategy. It's the basic foundation upon which our company rests." Bernard was Danone's head of marketing in 1990. Our Danone Institute commercials were made for him.

In 1998, Danone decided to consolidate all its advertising into one global network. Three major networks were consulted and, as an afterthought, so were we. The timing could not have been worse. We had been acquired but not yet merged with TBWA. In the end, we did not win the account. The decision was very hard to take, although I did understand. At the time, Young & Rubicam seemed much more solid globally than we were. They got the business.

From Yogurt to Microcredit

Frank Riboud's leadership of the corporation his father founded has been charismatic. He has launched many bold initiatives. He has completely transformed the group's structure. In particular, as I have already mentioned, he has refocused it around health-related activities, losing divisions and brands that did not fit in with this approach. He later bought Numico, a Dutch-based global leader in medical nutrition.

On another level, he has established a fruitful process of collaboration with Muhammad Yunus. I was struck, when reading Yunus's book, *Creating a World Without Poverty*, by the fact that the first chapter is entirely about his cooperation with Danone. It is entitled "Starting with a Handshake."

The story of social business and how the invention of microcredit has impacted the world is well known. Thanks to Muhammad Yunus, over the last quarter-century, more than six billion dollars have been distributed to millions of families. According to a recent study, some 64 percent of beneficiaries have managed to raise themselves above a condition of chronic poverty thanks to guarantee-free microcredit. "Financial logic has it that poor people should be pressured into repayment," Muhammad Yunus told Paris-based newspaper *Le Monde*. "At Grameen Bank, we do the opposite. We lend money without asking for guarantees. We do not impose exorbitant interest rates that keep people in a stranglehold. We have reversed the fundamentals of credit. With us, the less you own, the more we're interested." In this way, Yunus has helped millions of independent workers in developing countries—small shopkeepers, repair stores, or tailors—to set up their businesses. By abandoning the idea of guarantees, Muhammad Yunus has brought about the most fundamental disruption imaginable in financial spheres. He has shown that access to capital, even on a very small scale, can transform human lives. He has, as he says, tried to put an end to financial apartheid. He wants to find a place in the economic world for those 50 percent of human beings who earn less than two dollars a day.

When Franck Riboud and Muhammad Yunus set up Grameen Danone Foods, they invented the social multinational. In a social business, the people who put up the funding—the shareholders—recover their initial stake after a certain time, but no dividend is ever paid. Nevertheless social corporations are not charities. They function like any another company. They are bound to develop turnover to cover costs, whereas charities live entirely on donation. Muhammad Yunus is respectful of charity. But he also emphasizes its limitations, pointing out that there is such a thing as "compassion fatigue."

Grameen Danone Foods manufactures and sells very low-cost yogurt. It fills a nutritional gap: one yogurt provides 35 percent of the daily nourishment a person needs. Milk is transported from farm to village by little three-wheeled refrigerated vehicles. It is combined with locally grown sugar and other nutritional ingredients.

The resulting product is full of vitamins and other healthy elements. It is known in Bengali as "Shokti," which means energy. It is designed to stay fresh for one week because no one has a refrigerator in that part of the country. The production process takes place in a series of micro-plants in Bogra District. A rural distribution service is performed by fifteen hundred so-called "Shokti ladies" wheeling the yogurt around the countryside.

Danone learns insights every day from its experiences in low-income countries. As Franck Riboud puts it, "You learn to work in a different way in terms of logistics, product access and proximity…. In the end, it changes the way we do things in France. Usual practice is to send out expatriates to impose the way things are done back home in poorer countries. I want to establish the exact opposite. On a daily basis, I take decisions that affect people—consumers, children—who are often on the breadline. If I find a way for them to be able to buy, then I will certainly be in a position to better manage the demands of the hard discounters in France!"

It's been more than ten years since I last worked for this corporation. I was very attached to it. I thought I would never work for Danone again. Then one day I discovered that our office in Bangladesh is in charge of Danone. They even asked Muhammad Yunus to be the brand's spokesman in its advertising. You can see him in those commercials surrounded by dozens of children praising the merits of "Shokti" yogurt, and of social business. The children around gaze at him with a mixture of affection and respect. Muhammad Yunus may have made some enemies in political circles in his homeland, yet he remains a living god there.

The story has come full circle. I worked for Danone for a quarter-century. I was sad to see our collaboration come to an end. Now, one of the agencies in our network is helping Danone in its noblest endeavor.

Zimbabwe

"Can you send us a poster for our permanent collection?"

A British Museum curator sent this request to John Hunt, the head of our Johannesburg agency. He wanted to exhibit a visual from the campaign that won the most awards ever in the history of advertising. This was the campaign produced in 2009 for *The Zimbabwean* newspaper. John had to read the letter several times over. He was both flattered and moved that such a great London institution should consider his campaign a work of art in its own right. Above all, this demand represented the climax of an adventure that was to remain in the minds of South Africans, Zimbabweans, and bloggers the world over as the "Trillion-Dollar Campaign."

Trillion-Dollar Campaign

The Zimbabwean newspaper was established in 2005 after journalists were hounded out of their country for denouncing rigged elections. Robert Mugabe's regime had destroyed the opposition. It had also led Zimbabwe into chaos. A team of volunteers gathered around Wilf Mbanga, a well-known Zimbabwean publisher, and the newspaper was edited from London. As the slogan said, *The Zimbabwean* provided "a voice for the voiceless."

But back in the beginning, as is so often the case in Africa, everything had seemed to be going so well. The entire nation burst into collective joy when Zimbabwe was born in 1980. People danced to the sound of Bob Marley's *Zimbabwe*, a song written to celebrate the birth of the new state that had risen from the ruins of what used to be known as Rhodesia. Salisbury became Harare. Robert Mugabe, the prime minister, was elected president in 1987. Then everything went wrong. Mugabe ran a dictatorship, and turned himself into the tyrannical head of a regime based on terror and denunciation. In an interview with Paris's *Le Monde* newspaper, he had the gall to say he had a "degree in violence". What followed was unprecedented economic and social ruin. The man affectionately known to his friends in the resistance times as Comrade Bob, a national liberator, turned into Mugabe the despot. His twelve million fellow Zimbabweans entered a nightmarish era. There was unheard of distress. The land fell prey to famine and cholera. Hyperinflation took root. In 2008, the annual inflation rate reached an impossible to comprehend 231 million percent. The strong man of Harare thought he could best serve his own interests by printing money, and at this, he did not hold back.

As early as 1989, the opposition was dissolved. Reporters were put under surveillance. Those who were bold enough to denounce the regime's totalitarian inclinations were arrested, often beaten up and forced into exile. In June 2008, the regime imposed an import tax on newspapers printed abroad, payable in foreign currency. This trick was intended to muzzle an independent press by ensuring it could not get to locals. Foreign-based newspapers, such as *The Zimbabwean*, were classified as luxury products. Overnight, they became unaffordable to ordinary readers.

Three million Zimbabweans live in South Africa, their larger neighbor. Most are recent immigrants. One solution might be to encourage them to read the newspaper. The increase in sales would then help subsidize sales inside Zimbabwe. The publisher approached us for a plan of action. We recommended that he denounce economic waste in Zimbabwe by attacking the currency collapse. How could this be achieved at little cost? There was only just enough money to pay for a few posters. Our agency came up with an idea that would make history. Rather than print the posters on expensive paper, we decided to print them on now worthless Zimbabwean bank notes.... One by one, real bank notes were posted by hand on giant billboards.

One of the most eloquent symbols of the collapse of the Zimbabwean economy is a famous bank note: the hundred-thousand-billion-dollar note. A whole run of bank notes whose face value reached dizzying heights was issued, even though there was no monetary value to back them up. The hundred-thousand-billion-dollar note remains the highest face-value bank note ever issued. It no longer exists, but I am lucky enough to own one that I keep in my office. When it was first issued in 2009, this 100,000,000,000,000 dollar note—I haven't made a mistake, that's the actual number of zeros printed on the note—was worth about thirty US dollars. Most Zimbabwean bank notes were worth a lot less than the paper they were printed on. If these notes could neither buy anyone a loaf of bread nor, by the same token, an advertising campaign, they might as well be used for something. And that is how hundred-thousand-billion Zimbabwean dollar notes came to be used as the paper for the campaign to be printed on. Here are three of the slogans that were used, printed on the bank notes themselves:

"It's cheaper printing this on money than paper."
"250 million Zimbabwean dollars cannot buy the paper to print this poster on."
"Thanks to Mugabe, this money is wallpaper."

The resulting posters were like giant murals or frescoes on the major avenues in Johannesburg. Also, tens of thousands of bank notes were distributed at street corners, in malls, and universities as flyers, with the newspaper's e-mail address overprinted on them. Bank notes were also sent to businessmen, to politicians and media celebrities. No one was left out. No street corner was left unturned.

Thousands of worthless bank notes gave our "Trillion-Dollar Campaign" global prominence. As soon as the campaign began, it was talked about and commented upon on national TV and on every radio station. Soon, the whole world was able to access the posters via the Internet, which brought massive awareness at record speed. We achieved worldwide exposure. We were on the *New York Times* website, on the *Le Monde* website in France, on *Huffington Post*. There was coverage on more than eight hundred websites and blogs around the world. Dozens, maybe hundreds, of TV channels reported on what we were doing. More than two million hits were registered on *The Zimbabwean*'s website the week the campaign was launched.

This is what Wilf Mbanga, *The Zimbabwean*'s editor-in-chief, wrote about the idea: "Using the valueless currency was a stroke of genius. Nobody bothered to steal it! None of the posters or billboards were ever defaced—despite the fact that they were made of actual notes. This proved beyond doubt the worthlessness of the currency and the failure of the Mugabe regime to manage its economy." He also spoke of the campaign's "eloquent simplicity."

A few months later, the government in Harare was forced to enact a drastic measure. Pure and simple, it cancelled its currency. Every bank note in circulation was found and destroyed. The campaign had put the most powerful symbol of economic lunacy to death. The authorities did not even bother to establish a new currency. Today, two currencies operate inside

Zimbabwe: US dollars and South African rands. There is no local currency.

As for *The Zimbabwean*, its circulation increased within a few weeks by more than 50 percent. The government in Harare was forced to abolish its special levy on press imported from abroad. The paper was saved.

The Art of the Ephemeral

This campaign cost next to nothing. Only about twenty billboard sites in Johannesburg had been rented. The impact was global. In 2009, the posters won prizes in every major advertising festival, including Cannes, London, New York, and Singapore. John Hunt, the man behind this campaign, sums it up by saying the same thing he has been telling his teams for years: "It's not the size of your budget but the size of the idea that counts."

Recycling bank notes is a deliberate perversion of usage such as is found in contemporary art. Some of the flyers we produced have become collectors' items, since the bank notes themselves have vanished from circulation. When the curator at the British Museum called John Hunt to ask for campaign originals, he said, "We are looking for turning points in the history of contemporary art." He considered the campaign for *The Zimbabwean* a defining moment. Nothing could have given John Hunt more pleasure. A country has to give up its currency. A dictator is shown up around

312

ZIMBABWE

the world. An advertising campaign wins more prizes than any previous campaign in history. But to John, the British Museum means more than anything else. It's a consecration.

Advertising has been seen in museums for a long time, ever since Toulouse-Lautrec designed his posters for Paris's Moulin Rouge cabaret. More recently, the best advertising films have been screened in contemporary art museums. Art and advertising have for a long time conducted an incestuous relationship. Their meeting is often unpredictable but fertile. Absolut did not ask Warhol to paint its label. It was Warhol who suggested it, the first in an unlikely succession of artists of all sorts to show in the Absolut Museum in Stockholm. They include painters and musicians, sculptors and architects and fashion designers.

I am often asked whether advertising is an art. I always say that I have never believed that. But it is a discipline that has been transformed by artists. The greatest photographers, illustrators, directors, and screenwriters have ennobled it. Some people reiterate the question insistently. I concede then that advertising is perhaps an art of the ephemeral. It has no interest in posthumous success.

Success in advertising must be immediate. From day one, *The Zimbabwean* paper was saved.

313

Afterword

Disruption has been with me for twenty years. It is a concept that lies at the heart of what follows below.

In the world in which we now live, no single factor can be considered in isolation. Everything contributes to everything else. Everything depends on everything else. Never have individual lives been so dependent on collective destiny.

Intelligence itself has become collective. Inventors emerging out of the solitary confinement of their laboratories to bring us new ideas are a thing of the past. MIT researchers work increasingly in multidisciplinary teams. So do their colleagues in corporate R&D departments. Corporate strategy is no longer devised by lonely CEOs in ivory towers. More and more employees take part in a joint elaboration process.

As never before, the period to come will favor collective endeavors. We are entering into a world of interdependence, where the movement in our individual brains matters less than the movement from

315

one brain to the next. Being open to others will provide the foundation for individual inventiveness—and for future wealth creation.

Coming generations will need to define a new political geography. They will need to find a new balance between North and South. More harmonious work relations inside companies. New connections between public and private sectors. Between family life and social life.

More than ever, in the face of the obstacles ahead, in the face of the challenges we will encounter, the appropriate behavior will be to act disruptively. To constantly challenge convention. Merely extrapolating the future from what we know of the past won't be enough. We will need to discover solutions that today seem unimaginable.

The previously inconceivable must become part of our everyday lives. If ten years ago anyone had described what Apple, Google, or Facebook are offering us today, no one would have believed them. We must learn to think the unthinkable. It is only on this condition that we may hope to master this unpredictable world in which we live.

The time has come for us to be unrealistic. This is the best way to preserve what is real.

Nearly all the advertising campaigns discussed in this book were created by my partners at TBWA. I would like to thank them for all they did. And also the people from other agencies whose work I have mentioned.

Exhibit

Corporate History

Mergers and Acquisitions

1968:   Creation of Chiat\Day in Los Angeles

1971:   Creation of TBWA in Paris, which quickly obtained a presence throughout Europe and the United States following the acquisition of Costello & Fine.

1984:   Creation of BDDP in Paris, present throughout Europe, Asia, and the United States through the acquisition of Wells Rich Greene.

1991:   Acquisition of TBWA by Omnicom.

1995:   Acquisition of Chiat\Day by Omnicom. Merger with TBWA.

1998:   Acquisition of GGT/BDDP by Omnicom. Merger of BDDP and TBWA international networks.

2007:   TBWA ranked sixth largest worldwide network by *Advertising Age*.

Milestones

1989:   BDDP launches hostile takeover of BMP, quoted UK agency, including American agencies Ammirati & Puris, and Goodby, Berlin, Silverstein. Omnicom intervenes as White Knight and acquires agencies mentioned above.

1990:   BDDP acquires Wells Rich Greene. Saddled by debt, BDDP is acquired by GGT, quoted UK agency.

1998:   As indicated above, Omnicom acquires GGT/BDDP. The TBWA network, resulting essentially from the mergers of TBWA, Chiat\Day, and BDDP, takes definitive shape.

Notable Achievements

2004:   TBWA *Adweek* Network of the Year

2006:   TBWA *Advertising Age* Network of the Year

2008:   TBWA *Advertising Age* and *Adweek* Network of the Year

Acknowledgments

This book has been written in English and in French at the same time. I would like to give profound thanks to Pierre Hodgson, who was at my side phrase by phrase for the English version. His sense of nuance is incomparable, and without him, this book would not have existed as such.

I would also like to thank my old friend Nick Baum, who provided me with countless bits of advice, helped me to avoid making numerous mistakes, and above all contributed a great number of highly pertinent suggestions.

I am extremely fortunate to have Pamela Tamby as my assistant. Her guidance was precious and her support infallible.

Allow me also to mention all those who, in their own way, have helped to make this book what it is. In particular Emmanuel André, Djazia Boukhelif, Laure Chauvel, Nicole Cooper, Laurie Coots, Brune Diricq, Carolina Labi, Marie-France Lavarini, Rosanne

Leroy, Ayami Nakao Pelata, Fanny Valeyre, Nicolas Bordas, Gérard Cicurel, Pierre Gauthronet, Pascal Mariani, Patrick O'Neill, Guillaume Pannaud, Jean-Marie Prénaud, Dayva Savio, Philippe Simonet, Rob Schwartz, Jean-David Sichel, Marianne Stefanowicz, Elaine Stein, François Vogel, and of course my wife Marie-Virginie and my children.

Finally, I owe my all gratitude to Craig Cohen, Will Luckman, Lindsey Alexander and would also like to recognize powerHouse Books and all those there who participated in this book.